PUBLISHED BY

MADE POSSIBLE THROUGH THE GENEROUS SUPPORT OF

IN PARTNERSHIP WITH

Employees & Alumni Association
of the National Park Service

OH, RANGER!®

True Stories from our National Parks

EDITED BY

Mark J. Saferstein

©2007 APN Media, LLC
Published by American Park Network
1775 Broadway, Suite 622
New York, New York 10019
212.581.3380
www.AmericanParkNetwork.com

Contributing Editor: Kathy Dimont
Photo Editor: Joel Saferstein
Technical Editor: Ken Mabery
Editorial Coordinator: Christine Carter

Book Design: Michael Cohen
Graphic Designer: Leyla Heckrotte
Cover Illustrations: Heather Finney
Printed by: Oceanic Graphic Printing

First edition, 2007
Designed in the United States of America
Printed and bound in China
ISBN-10: 0-9787101-2-6
ISBN-13: 978-0-9787101-2-5
LCCN: 2007929804

If you'd like to share your own national park adventures,
*please submit your stories to **mark@americanparknetwork.com**.*
Please remember to include all your contact information.

This book is dedicated to all park rangers and National Park Service employees. Thank you for everything you do to preserve and protect our national treasures.

Table of Contents

Fire!

Forces of Nature

Science & Discovery

Life Changing Experiences

Foreword

MY FATHER, THE FATHER OF OUR NATIONAL PARKS
by Marian Albright Schenck

If you have any doubts left about your purpose, go live in a city and change your profession. Try to duplicate your way of life and the purpose for which you serve. You stand for something fine and lasting with your goal of preserving and caring for America's scenic and historic heritage.

Horace M. Albright addressing his beloved rangers at Ranger Rendezvous X in 1932.

On August 25, 1916, Congress passed the National Park Service Organic Act and a new idea was born. An agency would be created to conserve our nation's special places, the first of which was Yellowstone National Park—an area of land the size of Rhode Island and Delaware combined! My father, Horace Albright, became the first superintendent of Yellowstone. The National Park Service was to assume responsibility for the area from the United States Army. Facing so many new challenges, my father's primary concern was to protect the wondrous resources in his care and the people who came to enjoy them. The cavalry troops who had policed the park were gone. Who was going to take their place? He didn't have to look far.

Fortunately the Army had left behind an assortment of men who were separate from the regular corps. Most had originally served as scouts and packers in the so-called "horse wars"— the Spanish-American War and the Philippine Insurrection. They had moved the camp facilities as the military advanced. Later, in Yellowstone, they became valuable assistants to the Army as they familiarized themselves with the wilderness and worked alongside the soldiers.

My father had another valuable recruitment source. The seasoned cavalrymen leaving the park were offered a discharge if they stayed on to become rangers. A few did. Additional men

1

Herbert Hoover with Horace, Marian and Bob Albright (1927)

came from the ranks of the expert stagecoach drivers who had spent years hauling supplies to outlying facilities and showing tourists the breathtaking sights at Yellowstone.

Within a year or so, a permanent ranger force of about 30 men had been amassed, which by then included an even more varied assortment of characters: one from a road maintenance crew, another a pre-Prohibition bartender, some cowboys from local ranches and so forth. So how were these new employees of the National Park Service to be paid? After removing the Army, Congress, in its infinite wisdom, had neglected to provide money to pay the new personnel. Fate was kind and the automobile helped to provide the answer.

For the 1916 season, cars were to be permitted in Yellowstone. It was a giant step forward to accommodate transportation, lodging and, of course, the influx of tourists. After the end of World War I, a surge of civilians in their newly acquired autos raced to discover Yellowstone. The National Park Service adopted a slogan to promote the parks, "See America First." A fee of $7.50 per entrant was collected, which quickly took care of the shortfall. Congress soon understood the importance to budget for the necessary personnel in Yellowstone and rolled out other similar fee programs in the remainder of the "crown jewels" of our National Park System. Congress also realized the need for appropriations to safeguard the rangers, their housing and—in the larger parks—enough comforts that married men could bring their wives and children. By 1925, my father achieved another very important accomplishment. He persuaded Congress to extend Civil Service status to all rangers.

During the years that my father was superintendent, Yellowstone National Park was closed to visitors for about eight months of the year. The old saying was that there were four months of the year in the park—June, July, August and winter. In the months that the park was closed, he focused on his duties as assistant field director in Washington. These months were spent overseeing budget and congressional actions, decisions on roads, construction, acquisitions, personnel, policy, annual reports and so forth. He also served during the winters of 1926 to 1928 as temporary superintendent of Yosemite.

My father established standards for rangers throughout the system. From knowledge gained in his ten years in Yellowstone, working with the first ill-assorted, devoted rangers and the later college-educated men, he finalized the prerequisite standards of clothing, conduct, etc. Today, the requirements have evolved, as rangers have become more and more specialized. The following letter that was sent to prospective rangers in 1926 provides a wonderful insight into just how much has changed since the early days of the parks. At the same time, you'll see that many of the challenges rangers still face—to preserve and protect our national parks for future generations—have remained exactly the same.

Horace Albright at Camp Roosevelt in Yellowstone National Park (1925)

SUPERINTENDENT HORACE ALBRIGHT'S REPLY TO LETTERS
OF APPLICATION FOR SUMMER RANGER POSITIONS (1926)

We have received your letter indicating your desire to become a ranger in Yellowstone National Park for the season of 1926. Before giving further consideration, we ask you to read this circular letter very carefully and thoughtfully, and, if you are still interested in the ranger position after completing your study of this communication, fill out the enclosed blank and return it to the park headquarters with a picture of yourself.

It has been our experience that young men often apply for a place on the park ranger force with the impression or understanding that the ranger is a sort of sinecure with nothing resembling hard work to perform, and that a ranger's position offers an opportunity to pass a pleasant vacation amid the beauties and wonders of Yellowstone Park, and very frequent trips about the park and innumerable dances and other diversions to occupy one's leisure hours.

The conceptions of the duties of the ranger just mentioned are just as untrue as it is possible for them to be, and unfortunately the pay is so small that boys earning their way through college, and who live at a distance from the park cannot afford to become a ranger if tendered a place.

The pay is $100 a month. The successful applicant must pay his own traveling expenses to and from the park, and must subsist himself in the park. He must furnish his own clothes, including a uniform costing about $45. He must bring his own bed.

We make no promises regarding transportation around the park to see its wonders, and often rangers do not get a chance to see all of the park unless they can be granted leave from their duties and make their own arrangements for the trip. Men who render excellent service and are retained until the close of the season are given an opportunity to tour the park if facilities are available, otherwise not.

Applicants for a ranger's position must be 21 years of age or must attain that age by June 15th. If you are not 21 or will not be by June 15th, don't apply. If you have the reputation of appearing unusually youthful or immature for a man of 21, don't apply. We want men who are mature in appearance. We prefer men of 25 to 30 years of age.

The ranger is primarily a policeman, therefore he should be big in frame, tall, and of average weight for his age and height. We always prefer big men to small men, other conditions being equal. If you are small of stature, better not apply.

The ranger must have a pleasing personality; he must be tactful, diplomatic and courteous; he must be patient. If you are not possessed of such characteristics, please don't apply. Without them, you would become, if selected, a failure from the beginning of your service.

The ranger is often called upon to guide large parties of tourists and to lecture to them on the features of the park. He should have a good strong voice and some experience in public speaking. Detail public speaking experience and training on the application form.

The ranger must know how to cook ordinary foods and must have experience in kitchen police. If you cannot cook and care for a ranger station, don't apply. You would be an unpopular burden on your fellow ranger and the butt of all station jokes should you be selected without this essential qualification.

We want big, mature men with fine personalities and experience in the out-of-doors in riding, camping, woodcraft, fighting fires and similar activities.

Rangers must rise at 6:00 a.m. and must retire not later than 11:00 p.m. They may attend dances and other entertainment not more than two evenings a week. A ranger is on duty from the time he arises until he retires, and may even be called from his bed for emergency service. He is not subject to an 8-hour law, and he is not paid for services rendered in excess of an 8-hour period.

Carefully reflect on what you have just read. You have perhaps believed government jobs to be "soft" and "easy." Most of them are not, and certainly there are no such jobs in the National Park Service. Please do not return the enclosed blank unless you believe you are fully qualified and unless you mean business. Remember there is no vacation in the work, and mighty little money.

If you want a summer in the park as an experience in outdoor activity amid forests and a fine invigorating atmosphere, apply if you are qualified. Otherwise, please plan to visit the Yellowstone National Park as a tourist.

Horace M. Albright, Superintendent

Clearly an applicant for a ranger position—or any job in America—would never receive a letter like this today, but it was indicative of its time. Whoa! Don't forget, my father was also the first to appoint a woman to become a full time ranger, Miss Isabel Basett, who proudly donned the gray-green uniform in 1920.

Once the rangers were organized, their appearance, knowledge, conduct and pride in their position created an aura of respect that sometimes bordered on hero-worship among the park visitors. To get the attention of one of them, the most common call was "Oh, Ranger!"

During a brief lull in his winter inspections, my dad visited Frank Taylor, a well-known writer of articles for *The Saturday Evening Post, Colliers* and other popular magazines of that day. Frank had been suggesting that they combine forces to write a book about national parks. My father agreed. He produced an outline of proposed contents, provided the necessary data and proofread the various chapters Frank had whipped up. Frank also persuaded his sister, noted artist Ruth Taylor White, to contribute her clever cartoons (many of which have been reproduced on the opening and closing spreads of this book). When the two men had completed their undertaking, Stanford University offered to publish the book. *Oh, Ranger!* first appeared in 1928 and continued for many years, sometimes with new publishers, revisions and editions.

My dad was never very far from his rangers. He called them his "Greenies," for they were always on his mind and in his heart. He and I were writing a book at the time of his death (age 97 in 1987). He wrote the dedication in advance and it was thus inserted:

> *To "the Greenies"—the National Park Service rangers in the field,*
> *the dedicated hard-working, backbone spirit of the service.*

This book of ranger stories is an entirely new and different version of *Oh, Ranger!*, filled with wonderful stories from all across our system of national parks. My father's thoughts would be with these contemporary rangers. He would revel in sharing their adventures and experiences. I believe that, if he were here, he would like to pass on the same sentiments of support and encouragement today that he expressed in his farewell letter to National Park Service employees back in 1933.

HORACE ALBRIGHT'S FAREWELL LETTER TO
NATIONAL PARK SERVICE PERSONNEL (August 1933)

In this letter, perhaps one of my last official statements to you, let me urge you to be aggressive and vigorous in the fulfillment of your administrative duties. The National Park Service, from its beginning, has been an outstanding organization because its leaders, both in Washington and out in the field, have worked unceasingly and with high public spirit to carry out the noble policies and maintain the lofty ideals of the Service as expressed in law and executive pronouncement. Do not let the Service become "just another Government bureau;" keep it youthful, vigorous, clean and strong. We are not here to simply protect what we have been given so far; we are here to try to be the future guardians of those areas as well as to sweep our protective arms around the vast lands which may well need us as man and his industrial world expand and encroach on the last bastions of wilderness. Today we are concerned about our natural areas being enjoyed for the people. But we must never forget that all the elements of nature, the rivers, forests, animals and all things co-existent with them must survive as well.

I hope that particular attention will be accorded always to that mandate in the National Park Service Act of 1916 and in many organic acts of the individual parks, which enjoins us to keep our great parks in their natural condition. Oppose with all your strength and power all proposals to penetrate your wilderness regions with roads, motorways and other symbols of modern mechanization. Keep large sections of primitive country free from the influence of modern, destructive civilization. Keep these primitive bits of the America of the pioneer for those who seek peace and rest in the silent places; keep them for the hardy climbers of the crags and peaks; keep them for the horseman and pack train; keep them for the scientist and student of nature; keep them for all who would use their minds and hearts to know what God had created. Remember, once opened, they can never be wholly restored to primeval charm and grandeur.

I urge you to be ever on the alert to detect and defeat attempts to exploit commercially the resources of the national parks. Often these projects will be formulated and come to you "sugar-coated" with an alluring argument that the park will be benefited by its adoption. We national park men and women know that nature's work as expressed in the world-famous regions in our charge cannot be improved upon by man.

Beware, too, of innovation in making the parks accessible. For a half-century, elevators, cableways, electric railways and similar contrivances have been proposed form time to time and have been uniformly rejected. The airplane, while now an accepted means of transportation, should not be permitted to land in primitive places.

Park usefulness and popularity should not be measured in terms of mere numbers of visitors. Some precious park areas can be destroyed by concentration of too many visitors. We should be interested in the quality of park patronage, not by quantity. The parks, while theoretically are for everybody to use and enjoy, should be so managed that only those numbers of visitors that can enjoy them, while at the same time not overuse and harm them, would be admitted at a given time. We must keep elements of our crowded civilization to a minimum in our parks. Certain comforts, such as safe roads, sanitary facilities, water, food and modest lodging, should be available. Also extra care must be taken for the children, the elderly and the incapacitated to enjoy the beauty of the parks.

We have been compared to the military forces because of our dedication and esprit de corps. In a sense this is true. We do act as guardians of our country's land. Our National Park Service uniform, which we wear with pride, does command the respect of our fellow citizens. We have the spirit of fighters, not as a destructive force, but as a power for good. With this spirit, each of us is an integral part of the preservation of the magnificent heritage we have been given, so that centuries from now people of our world, or perhaps of other worlds, may see and understand what is unique to our earth, never changing, eternal.

Animal Encounters

The Gentleman Bear
- SEQUOIA NATIONAL PARK -

Trouble at Alligator Pond
- TIMUCUAN ECOLOGICAL AND HISTORIC PRESERVE -

Dolphin Rescue
- CANAVERAL NATIONAL SEASHORE -

Flying Cubs
- CRATER LAKE NATIONAL PARK -

Skunk!
- PICTURED ROCKS NATIONAL LAKESHORE -

The Huckleberry Trail
- GLACIER NATIONAL PARK -

Brutus the Bear
- WHISKEYTOWN NATIONAL RECREATION AREA -

The National Park System preserves some of the most diverse natural ecosystems in the world. Our parks are home to a myriad of plant and animal species; some not found anywhere else on earth.

Stories about animal encounters in parks are endless. If you're lucky, you may see bison, bears, moose, wolves, mountain lions, elk, deer, antelope, coyotes, alligators, mountain goats or caribou to name a just a few. Birds abound, including bald eagles—a majestic symbol of our great nation. In coastal or island parks, whale watchers are rewarded with frequent sightings, while dolphins, seals, sea lions, sharks, octopi, coral and many other kinds of sea life flourish. There are untold thousands of smaller creatures: bobcats, badgers, wolverines, weasels, foxes, beavers, bats, mice, chipmunks, rabbits, lizards, frogs, snakes and more—all are at home in our national parks and all contribute to the delicate balance of natural ecosystems.

Animals in national parks are wild, unpredictable and potentially deadly. They roam freely, while humans are just temporary visitors to their homes. Animals in nature don't behave like cartoon characters or trained circus animals. Visitors to national parks must recognize the risks involved with approaching wildlife. Rangers spend many hours explaining just how ferocious those sweet-looking animals can be. Bears are particularly challenging— some of them are even able to outsmart the rangers! Many years ago at Glacier National Park in Montana, a mother bear was seen teaching her cubs how to break into cars. She had discovered that with one hard push in just the right spot, the windshield would pop out of its frame, allowing easy access to the food inside. At Yosemite National Park in California, rangers observed that if a bear found food in a certain type of car, it would break into others of the same model!

Unfortunately, animals that rely on human food lose their natural ability to survive in the wild. This is true not only for bears, but for all animals. Once accustomed to human food, animals are especially dangerous because they lose their natural fear of people. Situations have been documented in which deer and bears have knocked people down in an effort to get food. This aggressive behavior works! People, reacting in terror, quickly give up their backpacks and picnic baskets. The animal gets the food and learns that a little aggression will yield an easy meal. This leads to one of the worst parts of a ranger's job—when he or she must kill an animal that has become overly aggressive and dependent on human food, posing a threat to the safety of the visitors.

In the early days of the national parks, rangers intentionally fed animals as a means of entertaining visitors. Now considered unthinkable, the practice of feeding bears was once routine. Every night, refuse trucks would rumble away from the restaurants, loaded with leftover food. Bleachers were set up where people would sit and wait for the trucks, which dumped their loads into pits. They called them "bear salads." People loved watching the bears, which, after generations, became "beggar bears," expecting park rangers and visitors to provide their food.

The good news is that we're constantly learning and revising our management practices. As soon as rangers realized how harmful it was to feed the animals, they took the very unpopular step of stopping the practice. By then, many bears no longer knew how to survive in the wild. It took a long time and a great deal of effort to undo the damage we'd caused. The situation is getting better. Rangers have worked hard to educate people about keeping food away from bears. Campgrounds are patrolled frequently and campfire programs include warnings about bears, food and safety. Specially designed bear-proof garbage cans and dumpsters were developed. Videos play on continuous loops in visitor centers and hotel lobbies, reinforcing safe practices. Backcountry campers can rent lightweight, sturdy bear-proof canisters that keep food locked away from wily bears. It was a hard lesson, but we now know that feeding wild animals destroys the essence of what makes them wild. Only by allowing nature to take its course will wild animals remain strong.

The most interesting stories about wild animals often come from chance encounters. Hikers have turned a bend in a trail to find a grizzly bear ambling along right in front of them. Photographers who have waited quietly for hours to take the perfect picture stumble across the shot of a lifetime on the way back to the lodge. Campers, even after following every safety rule, have awakened to find a large animal rummaging through their camp. So be prepared! Always consult with a ranger for safety tips, whether you're venturing out on a day hike or camping in the backcountry.

Everyone must do their part to help sustain the wild animals of our national parks. Love them by leaving them alone. Never approach any wild animal, no matter how tempting. Slow down when driving through our parks! Speed kills thousands of animals every year. Remember, you're in their home, so be respectful. Take photos from a safe distance. Only if we allow animals to be wild will they remain healthy and continue to be one of the most captivating attractions in our national parks for generations to come.

The Gentleman Bear

by Earnest "Scotty" Scott

During my 25 years as a national park ranger, I had occasion to be in contact with many types of bears, some bad and some not so bad. One bear, in particular, caused quite an uproar when he meandered into Cedar Grove at Sequoia-Kings Canyon Park.

Blackie was a Gentleman Bear; his only rummaging targets were the rangers' garbage cans. He would pass on by the campground garbage cans, though they were a mile closer than the housing area of the government employees. We lived in small camp trailers at the time. Many a night old Gentleman Bear would rub on the trailers, as he rather enjoyed scratching himself. He rubbed so hard that he rocked the trailer! Sometimes he came through camp during daylight hours. We would sit on the porch just to watch this 300-pound bear with a wonderful disposition clamber around. He even dressed like a gentleman. With a big white spot on his throat, it was as if he were wearing a bow tie.

With the coming of fall, our Gentleman Bear was getting hard-pressed for something to eat. An outfitter who provided pack animals (mostly burros) for the backpackers had hired a lady cook from Montana. Her quarters were out near the mess hall, which had screened half-walls on the sides and doors at both ends. Blackie made it his common practice to tear through the screens in the cooking area and easily locate and wipe out a month's worth of grub in a matter of minutes! It's no surprise, as bears have a fantastic sense of smell. It's been said that they can smell right through a tin can!

The outfitter soon alerted me about their problem. As a ranger, it's my duty to ensure the safety of everyone within our park. A hungry bear wandering around camp—even a gentleman bear like Blackie—is not safe for anyone, especially if he's become

MARC MUENCH

Sequoia National Park

accustomed to people and people food. So I set a bear trap, but Blackie was just too smart. Some bears are so intelligent that it gets them into trouble. It's as if they can put two and two together to get four.

In order to trigger the trap, the bait required a tugging action from the targeted intruder, which would cause the door to quickly close, locking the bear in the cage. Wouldn't you know it; Blackie would go in and push on the food, eating it right off the trigger! After he ransacked the cookhouse for the third time, something more had to be done, so I came up with what turned out to be a "hare-brained" idea.

The hunters and the guides were all in on it. The plan was as follows: An old broken down divan made its post in the entry of the mess hall. I planned to load up a shotgun and spread a sleeping bag on the divan, not to sleep, but to keep warm since it was bitterly cold. Then, I would place the shotgun on the floor, with the barrel pointing toward the kitchen area, poised and ready for our intruder. I would lie in the sleeping bag until I heard the old bear stumbling in, then roll out, grab the shotgun and, if he didn't get caught in the trap, I'd blast him! Of course, shooting old Blackie was a last resort. (Today, the use of weapons is strictly controlled and rangers would likely use tranquilizer darts in a similar situation.)

Well, Murphy's Law was in full force that night. I turned the sleeping bag inside out, so the zippers were inside. I did this because I thought it best to quietly unzip my compartment from the inside, rather than poking my arms out in plain sight of Blackie, thus informing him of my presence. Clothed in warm attire and wrapped in a toasty sleeping bag, I was ready to go. I settled in for a long wait. Problem was, I became so warm and comfortable that I fell asleep!

I awakened to the sounds of crunching and munching not more than ten feet from my head. When I went to pull on that zipper, it was jammed, and that's the God's honest truth!

The Gentleman Bear heard my struggles. Upon discovering he was not alone, he panicked! Without a moment's hesitation, he took off running. Instead of barreling through the door—an open route to the wilderness—or charging directly at me, he busted straight through the wall, leaving a gaping hole, just like a cartoon character! Bits of the wall shattered everywhere. I was now sitting up, still fully encased by the sleeping bag, which held me captive during the whole debacle. Upon hearing all the ruckus, the hunters came screaming through the door. There I sat in the lantern glow, trussed up like a mummy! As they helped me out of my own trap, the relentless ribbing began.

"Good plan, Scotty," they laughed, "Your plan caused more damage than the bear!" I spent the following day rebuilding the side of the cook shack and doing my best to also repair my slightly bruised ego.

At this point I was up a creek and desperately needed a new plan. I happened to be in the fire cage one day, going through the supplies, when I came across a big can of crushed pineapple. Aha, an idea! I grabbed the pineapple and a small canvas sack, filling the sack with pineapple. I used baling wire to tie this fruity bundle to the trigger on the trap. That bothersome bear was going to have to tear the sack open to get the pineapple! That would surely trigger the trap. I then strategically sprinkled some bits and juice leading into the trap.

The Gentleman Bear entered the cage and pulled hard to get that sack open. Whammy! The door swung closed.

As the day wore on, the sun warmed the air. The bear cautiously peered out through the door sniffing the air and smacking his dehydrated lips. I thought Blackie might appreciate some water, so I took a hose and sprayed the water inside the trap to cool him down. The liquid collected in the corrugations at the bottom of the trap providing him with a drink. Instead of lapping up the pools of water, or even tearing at the hose like most bears would, he just lay there with his mouth open drinking right out of the hose, like a real gentleman!

After calling on the radio asking for a crew to come and haul him off to somewhere safe, I positioned myself behind the ranger shack, keeping a close watch on our captive. Help arrived in the form of two fireguards with a pickup truck; both of them were "late seasonals" without too much experience. I handed over the bear in the trap to the fellows from Grant Grove for them to take Blackie deep into the wilderness, hoping I'd never see him again. I went back about my regular duties until I heard stressed voices over the radio.

Apparently, Blackie wasn't through with us just yet!

"The wheel came off what?!" the district ranger's voice crackled through the speaker.

"The bear trap! And it's got a bear in it!" the fireguards answered in a panic.

Not only did we have an immobile bear trap with a bear inside, this wheel had taken off cross-country, making a beeline toward a brand new Lincoln Continental! The wheel headed right for that car as if it had a target on its side. The driver of this shiny new vehicle must have heard that wheel tumbling toward her because she jumped out of the way, just in time to see the wheel crash into the door!

After calming the woman who owned the freshly dented car and doing a little crowd control, I helped get the wheel back on the trailer. I assured the men that the Gentleman Bear was good-natured and didn't deserve to be "dispatched." Since Blackie no longer posed an immediate threat, they agreed. Before they headed for the mountains, they marked old Blackie with yellow paint. This way, if he returned, everyone would know immediately that he was a "repeat offender," at which point he would have posed a serious risk to the safety of park visitors and employees. The fireguards took that troublesome bear to Redwood Mountain to turn him loose, far away from the cookhouse in Cedar Grove. Thankfully, I never saw old Blackie again!

I learned one very important lesson from my experience with Blackie the Gentleman Bear: crushed pineapple and a canvas sack can help a ranger outsmart a bear, as long as a stuck zipper doesn't first outsmart the ranger!

Trouble at Alligator Pond

by Craig Morris

The Theodore Roosevelt area of the Timucuan Preserve is a tract of second growth northeast Florida wilderness. It is surrounded by urban sprawl of close to a quarter million people. Yet less than thirty thousand visitors come to walk these wild trails each year. Those who do know that they are the few and fortunate. For within this "Emerald Isle" are nine distinct natural communities, each featuring animals and plants unique to their habitat. Yet only one animal can be found in all these natural communities: the American alligator. One late summer's day an alligator found me and it almost cost me my life.

I was on a routine patrol near a place called Alligator Pond, which has earned its name for good reason! It was an overcast day, late in August, as I strolled by the pond. I was focused on the egret rookeries in the small trees all around me. Every year I looked forward to visiting this area to see its innumerable birds. The young birds and the symbiotic relationship that existed between the egrets and alligators fascinated me. Alligator mating season in northeast Florida usually begins around April. Females build a mound of soil, vegetation and natural debris and lay an average of 32 to 46 eggs that take roughly two months to hatch. The mother 'gators fiercely guard their nests and

rarely stray far from them. This is why egrets and other wading birds choose to nest near or in ponds where alligators nest. The alligators swim below the bird's nests, and if a raccoon attempts to climb into the aquatic trees, the alligator attacks.

As I was walking, I suddenly spied a large conical pile of leaves and thought to myself, "what would anyone on our staff be doing raking up leaves all the way out here?" Two seconds later my native Floridian instincts kicked in and I realized that I was standing inches away from a large alligator's nest. Before I had time to react, an eight-foot-long angry female 'gator came charging out of the pond just a few feet away. There was nowhere to run, so I began climbing the nearest tree. I got most of my body up into the tree's branches but this protective mother lunged and grabbed the tip of my left foot in her tooth-filled mouth. We began a tug of war (tug of life as far as I was concerned), which ended with her ripping my shoe off and causing a nasty cut on my big toe.

Out of breath and bleeding, I watched her powerful upper jaw chomp down, toss and then swallow my government-issued shoe! I couldn't believe what had just happened. I felt embarrassed and a little bit idiotic. "Please, please don't let a visitor see me up the tree in this predicament," I muttered to myself. I had lived with alligators all my life. I had encountered them too many times to remember without ever being attacked. Yet, as soon as I let my guard down, it happened.

I snapped back to reality when the momma 'gator made a futile lunge up the tree, her 400 pounds smashing into the trunk. She struck with such incredible force that every branch, twig and leaf shook, along with every fiber of my body! Then I saw the "Birders," an elderly couple decked out in their safari gear, binoculars as thick as wine bottles, and the ever present bulge of a birders guide inside each of their vests. "Folks, I'd stay away from this side of the pond. Got one real mad momma 'gator below me." I yelled.

"You OK?" the man replied.

"Yep, as long as I stay right up here where I am." Their giant binoculars trained on me like something from NASA and the man called out again.

"Your foot is bleeding! Are you sure you're OK?"

"It's just a cut, I'm fine. Nothing hurt but my pride."

"You want us to come and distract her for you?" he said, sounding like he watched one too many TV shows about adventure in the Australian Outback.

"No sir! This area is swarming with 'gators, so please keep your distance. I'm more concerned for your safety than my own. I'll radio headquarters and get some rangers out here right away. Thanks anyway!"

Indeed, more and more 'gators on the lily pad-covered pond seemed to be looking in my direction, but none seemed bigger that this dragon below me, so I focused on her, trying to figure a way out of this mess. Her nest lay about 15 feet away to the left

CARL WALSH

Timucuan Ecological and Historic Preserve

and the only escape was the trail leading away from the tree to my right. I took off the other shoe and tied it to a branch. Now barefooted I felt more comfortable. I'm a native Floridian—going barefoot is a way of life. My feet were callused and I enjoyed my skin touching the earth. It's as though I could better feel nature's pulse. I'd tried to explain this concept to my supervisors but they made me wear backcountry footgear nonetheless. In hindsight, it's a good thing because otherwise that 'gator might have gotten some toes to eat instead of my shoe. For now, I figured if I had to make a run for it, which seemed inevitable, two bare feet were better than a shoe and a bare foot.

All of a sudden my radio crackled "305, copy?"

"305, copy," I replied. "Time to face the music," I said to the 'gator with a shrug. Then began the hilarious radio traffic between the two other rangers and me.

"Craig where are you?"

"Sitting in a tree near Alligator Pond," I replied dryly.

"What are you doing up a tree?" came the response.

"Bleeding." I replied, somewhat sarcastically.

Another deeper sounding voice chimed in, "Very funny. Now what's really happening, you've been gone over two hours!"

"Just what I told you! Look, a momma 'gator just bit my left foot and ate my shoe. So I climbed the nearest tree and here I sit."

"Where's the gator now?"

"At the base of the tree trunk staring at me. She's a good-sized one, eight or nine feet long I guess," I replied.

"Do you need assistance?" the younger, higher pitched ranger replied in a forceful voice.

I couldn't believe it! Did he just say what I thought he said? "Keep it professional," I told myself. This radio traffic is open for all to hear, no time for more sarcastic remarks. They'll probably come like a flood after all this is over. But I couldn't help myself... "Nah, I'll just stay put a few more hours, or days, 'til she's through hissing and lunging up the tree trunk... of course I need help you knuckleheads!" That's what we get for hiring people who are used to moose and porcupines, and not creatures left over from the dinosaur age.

"On my way to assist you, Craig," the voice cracked.

It's a good 40-plus minute walk from the park visitor center to Alligator Pond, so I just looked down at the 'gator and waited. "Remember "Alligator 101," Craig," I muttered to myself. Alligator 101 is my nickname for an excellent pamphlet published by The Florida Fish and Wildlife Conservation Commission entitled *Living with Alligators*. It's a brochure all people living in Florida should read because it is estimated that there are almost two million alligators in this state. Lesson number one now came back to mock me, "Attacks may occur when people do not pay close enough attention their surroundings when working or recreating near water." A little less than an hour later a ranger appeared gun in hand.

"Put that away," I growled.

"But what if I have to shoot her in self defense?" he replied.

"Good grief," I thought, "I'm the one in danger... What I need you to do is make a little distraction, just enough to get her away from the tree so I can jump down and make a run for it. Come closer. You'll be fine, she won't go very far from her nest," I coached.

"Whoopee, she's a big one!" he nervously remarked as he finally got the situation in full view. She had calmed down a bit and seemed not to even notice the other ranger's presence.

"See this big pile of leaves and vegetation to my left? That's her nest. Pick up some branches and try throwing them in that direction, but don't hit the nest. All I need is for her to move in that direction."

"Want me to fire off a few rounds and see if that works?" he asked.

"No, that will just upset the rookery. See that decayed pine knot to your right? Throw that into the pond just to the side of her nest." Splash! And she whipped around in that direction. That was all I needed. My feet hit the ground and my toes dug into the soil like a runner's cleats.

"She didn't even notice you!" the ranger said in astonishment. "That took some guts."

"Hey nice throw," I breathlessly replied. "I hope that never happens again..." Well, two years later it did. That time it was my right shoe, but that's another story.

Dolphin Rescue

by Laura E. Henning

It started out a dreary, gray Saturday morning at Canaveral National Seashore. Not at all the sunshiny day that visitors expect when they come to east central Florida to see our 57,000 acres of pristine coastline and barrier island lagoon system. That day the beach was quiet and there were almost no boaters on Mosquito Lagoon. It looked to be one of those quiet days that park rangers sometimes need to get our paperwork done. As I sat down at my desk to look at next month's activity schedules, I was interrupted by one of the park's law enforcement rangers. He had just gotten a phone call from two fishermen on the lagoon, where a baby bottlenose dolphin was repeatedly trying to beach itself. They didn't know quite what to do. Wow! An opportunity to help rescue a dolphin! This got me away from my desk in an instant!

Before running out the door, we called Sea World of Orlando and notified them of the situation, as they are the closest help for stranded marine mammals. We would call again by cell phone once we were on the location to update them on the situation.

We arrived at a spot on west side of Mosquito Lagoon, where the fishermen had parked and were wade fishing. We spoke to them and found out that they had seen a pod of Atlantic bottlenose dolphins feeding in the area. When the pod had moved out of

sight, they noticed that the calf was accidentally left behind. The calf was in knee-deep water and was very scared. It was only about two to three feet long. The fishermen had tried to take it back out into deeper water but it kept coming back to shore. We contacted the rescuers from Sea World and described the situation. They said to get in the water with the calf and try to keep it calm and keep it from hurting itself.

LAURENCE PARENT

Canaveral National Seashore

In a flash, I was in the water—uniform, boots and all—with my arms wrapped around the little calf. It let me hold its body. I cradled it as I walked to deeper water, where it was easier to keep the calf close to me. While walking I noticed that the calf still had the creases in its side that showed how it was curled up inside its mother. We knew that this was a very young dolphin that desperately needed to be with its mother. It had rubbed itself raw by running up onto the rough sand, so I cupped my hand underneath to keep it from further injury. I knelt down in the water and gently laid the calf down on my left side, keeping my hand underneath. It got a little anxious and I tried to keep it close to my body to make it feel secure. We knew that it needed to stay wet and out of the sun; even with the clouds dolphins are subject to severe sunburn. The calf calmed down and wrapped its tail around my back and tucked its snout under my knee. I stayed in this position while waiting for the experts from Sea World to arrive. As we got used to each other the calf lifted its head out of the water to take breaths and blow through its blowhole. I was careful not to restrict its movement too much and just hold on tight enough to make it feel secure. We started to get used to each other, so I began to feel around to see if there were any injuries that would give us a clue about why it was in this predicament. It let me run my fingers around on the inside of its mouth and I could feel that it did not have teeth yet. That meant that the calf was nursing and really needed help fast.

Sea World had said to sit tight until they arrived. It was an hour-and-a-half trip, once they got their rescue crew together. So there we sat. I patted and rubbed its slick, soft skin and it stayed put, with its snout tucked under my knee. I began to lose feeling in my legs, as I had been in this position for about an hour. I hardly even noticed. I was so enthralled with the feeling of being so close and connected to this beautiful little dolphin.

We kept an eye on our watches to try and gauge when the Sea World people would arrive. Close to two hours had passed. All of a sudden our little friend started getting restless. Its tail started swishing back and forth and it brought its head up and looked from side to side. There was a definite difference in its behavior and I tried my best to calm it down. I rubbed its side and spoke softly, doing everything I could to be reassuring. The next thing I knew, it gave two strong beats of its tail and swam away. We were all alarmed and thought it might return to the beach like it had earlier.

We watched as it swam around and then off just a little way in the distance we saw what the calf must have heard. It was the pod of dolphins coming toward us. The little calf left us without a backward glance and was once again with its family. Now we were left standing in the water trying to figure out exactly what we had witnessed. To the best of our knowledge, and by piecing it together with information from the folks at Sea World (who arrived shortly after the pod reappeared), we decided that the pod had been so busy and involved with rounding up the schooling bait fish and eating that they simply lost track of the calf. The calf, being so newly born, did not have the training or strength to keep up with the pod and somehow got left behind. After the feeding frenzy had died down and the dolphins had time to slow down and take notice, the calf's mother must have realized that her baby was missing. As soon as they realized their mistake, they returned to reclaim their lost little one.

While the nice people from Sea World ultimately made the trip for nothing, everyone was happy with the way things turned out. The dolphin would surely be better off with its mother than it ever could be in captivity, which also made for a much happier ending to my story. Every time I see a school group visiting the park on a field trip, I watch the teacher doing a head count of the children and remember that little dolphin. We know that dolphins are very intelligent and use certain thought processes to solve problems. I can only imagine what went through the mother dolphin's mind as she searched for her little calf. Maybe the calf was somehow able to let her know that a strange being in a green and grey uniform took good care of it while she was gone—just like we would for little lost humans!

Flying Cubs

by William "Mac" Brock

Crater Lake National Park gets a lot of snow, usually about 40 feet over the course of a winter. And the snow lingers well into the spring. Plows and blowers remove the snow from the roads, but the work leaves a corridor of ten-foot-high snow walls. The effect is a bit like driving through a tunnel without a roof. It works well for people and cars, but not as well for some of the animals. The plowed corridors can pose significant obstacles to their travel and getting trapped by the walls of snow puts them at great risk of getting hit by a passing vehicle.

Most animals have adapted well to the severe Oregon winters at Crater Lake and move about freely on top of the snow. Others simply move to lower elevations. Some of the unlucky ones get stuck on the plowed roads and find themselves unable to escape. For example, the more agile animals, such as squirrels and martens, eventually find a place where they can launch themselves up and over, but the less athletic porcupines sometimes need our help.

As a result, rangers are not surprised when notified that some wayward critter has gotten stuck on a road and is unable to get up and over the wall of snow. This was the case one night when I got called to help an animal in just this predicament. I was at

home with my family when a visitor came by after dinner to let me know that two bear cubs were stranded in the snow corridor. The cubs and their mother must have awakened early from their long winter's nap and went out to have a look around. Mom knew better than to go down onto the road, but the adventurous cubs had slid down the steep snow bank. According to the visitor's report, mama bear was on top of the snow bank, frantic

MARC MUENCH

Crater Lake National Park

with worry, while her cubs appeared scared to death, ten feet lower on the road and unable to climb back up. To compound the problem, the road still had a significant amount of traffic and motorists were inadvertently herding the frightened cubs ahead in their headlights. The cubs, in their efforts to dodge traffic, ran down the road, away from their mother and into the night.

This was the first time I'd ever encountered such a situation. Without the help of the tranquilizing drugs and darts one sees on TV, I donned my uniform jacket and my only personal protective equipment—my fire gloves—and set out to find the hapless cubs. Very soon one black ball of fur came running out of the night toward me. Without really thinking, I grabbed the little rascal and secured it under my arm like a lively football. Its sharp little teeth and claws dug into whatever it could reach, and my jacket, gloves and no small amount of skin were soon all cut up and worse for the wear. Holding on for dear life, I soon saw the sibling heading our way, so I grabbed it, too, and placed it under my other arm.

I obviously had no plan. I found myself wrestling with the two squirming cubs, who by now had found out that my fire gloves were really no match for their needle-sharp teeth. One would bite and the other bawl while we walked up the road to look for their mama. The report had said that she was still somewhere high up on the snow bank. Then I remembered what we always tell our visiting public: "Bears are wild animals; enjoy them from a distance and NEVER GET BETWEEN A SOW AND HER CUBS!" What was I thinking?! This was the dumbest move I'd ever made in my entire career, possibly in my entire life. Protecting wildlife is a huge part of my job and I just couldn't let these little guys fend for themselves on the road, where they would surely have been run over and killed.

With my heart in my throat, my mind fast-forwarded to the accident report that would surely be written if I continued to try to find the mama bear. I could envision the headline: Ranger Mauled While Trying To Save Two Bear Cubs! What a predicament! I reconsidered my course of action and decided that I must quickly help the cubs back onto the top of the snow bank and let them find their mother on their own. But which side of the road was mom on? If I put them on the wrong side they would be separated by a 40-foot-wide abyss and would probably try to cross again to find their mother. So, biting, clawing, bawling cubs and all, I walked on, looking for a clue about which side they had come from. My mind kept flashing to mama bear, and what she'd do if she saw me from the top of the snow bank, holding her terrified cubs. I pictured her charging down with the unbridled fury of a protective wild animal and the added advantage of higher ground. My knees started to shake and my resolve wavered, but just then I found where the cubs had slid down the embankment. Thankfully, I hadn't encountered mom! We weren't out of trouble yet. I tried, but just couldn't climb the steep slope with both cubs tucked under my arms. So after a moment's pondering, I did the only thing I could. With a mighty heave, I tossed one bawling cub up in the air, sailing over my head and onto the snow bank above. Just as I wound up and let fly with cub number two, a car drove up and illuminated the area. The cub was spread eagled in mid-flight, sailing up and over the snow bank right after its sibling. The visitors drove up with confused and worried looks on their faces, clearly trying to decipher what they had just seen. "Just some kids out after curfew, folks!" I explained.

I was still unsure about whether the cubs had actually been reunited with their mother that night but the next day the family was sighted together. I can only hope they were headed back to their den for the rest of the winter!

Skunk!

by Larry Kangas

I was a field ranger at Pictured Rocks National Lakeshore during the late 1980s. On a warm summer afternoon, the lifeguard received a frantic report from a swimmer and called me on the radio to report that a skunk was inside the swim beach changing house. He wanted me to come get it out!

When I first became a ranger, "skunk patrol" was not one of the first things that came to mind when thinking about my job description. Frankly, this seemed like a reasonable task for a fit, young lifeguard who was trained to save human lives. Unfortunately, he simply refused. He wanted me, the protection ranger, to take care of it. Like my fellow rangers, each day when we put on our green and grey uniforms and don our flat hats, there's no telling what's in store. So I headed off to the beach area to see what fate awaited me.

The changing room is a small, plain, one-room building, with wrap-around benches inside. There's a doorframe but no door. The skunk, like the park visitors, could come and go freely. For some reason it had gone in and wouldn't come out. Despite the spartan fixtures, the skunk seemed to really like that changing house. As you could imagine, this had the opposite effect on the park's human visitors! I knew this would end up being a smelly job if not done right. People would be able to tell for days—without even looking—who was on the losing end of this encounter.

During my earlier days as a backcountry ranger, my wife and I, and Amy, our one-year-old daughter, lived out of a tent for three months. We had many experiences with skunks, mostly one skunk in particular, none of which turned out too badly. Every evening, a skunk would saunter through our campground in search

LAURENCE PARENT

Pictured Rocks National Lakeshore

of scraps of food that people had inadvertently dropped on the ground or left behind. We were accustomed to seeing the skunk, as it would come to our site and go under our picnic table, right underneath Amy's child seat, which fit directly onto the tabletop. Our uninvited guest seemed to always know all the best spots to pick up an easy meal. (Amy always managed to drop lots of good tidbits.) Whenever the skunk appeared, we would sit still and quiet so as not to alarm it. Eventually, it would move off to the next campsite and we would soon hear the campers scream "SKUNK!" and then start running away. The skunk ruled!

As I approached the changing house, I recalled from my early training how important it is to not startle a wild animal. (That goes for all wild animals, big and small.) So I started talking in a soft manner to the yet unseen skunk. I knew that to keep the job from smelling, I needed to be calm and as non-threatening as possible. The defensive belt strapped securely around my waist—with my gun, mace and baton—certainly didn't hold the right tools for this job! No, for this job, I was going to rely on a calm, steely resolve, mixed with an equal portion of good luck.

Once inside the doorway, I saw the skunk crouched down underneath the bench in the back of the small room. It appeared normal and healthy, which was a good sign. (A scraggily looking creature might be more aggressive and would also be more likely to harbor disease.) I kept talking softly to the little fellow as I slowly entered the changing room. My hope was that if I walked very slowly toward it, then the skunk would calmly move away from me and exit the building. I was banking on the fact that he didn't want to have anything to do with me, any more than I did with him. I hugged the right side as I entered to give it as much space as possible on the opposite side of the small room. I knew I needed to make sure he didn't feel trapped and that I left an easy escape route.

A quarter of the way into the building, it started to move to my left. So far, so good. When I got to the back of the building the skunk was standing directly between me and the door—only about eight feet away and blocking my only exit. I realized that I was trapped in the worst possible position. If the skunk decided to unload, I had nowhere to go. I would be fully covered by its natural defenses and the concrete, windowless walls and low ceiling would hold all that stink in, making it more concentrated and potent than ever. Despite my predicament, or rather because of it, I continued to talk to him in a calm manner, telling him he could go out, that everything was going to be all right. (Perhaps I was talking to myself as well!) Upon reaching the door he hesitated, looked me up and down one last time, then turned and ran quickly into the woods. I was immediately relieved and came out smelling like a rose. (OK, at least not smelling like a skunk.) I had saved the day and provided a memorable experience for a small group of swimmers, and one very relieved lifeguard.

The Huckleberry Trail

by Bill Schustrom

The greatest symbol of wilderness today is the grizzly bear. To see one of the great bears from your car or along a mountain trail instills a sense of awe and respect. The grizzly has no natural rivals in wilderness areas. Their size, strength and speed place them on top of the food chain. The grizzly has earned our respect since the time of Lewis and Clark. Americans Indians had warned the explorer about the powerful creatures, but Lewis remained unimpressed until he had his own close encounter.

Many of our national parks have bears and Glacier National Park is no exception. It is estimated that within our one million acres there are close to 300 grizzly bears and almost twice as many black bears. Our park has over 700 miles of hiking trails, so there is always a chance for folks to encounter a bear while hiking. Bears can be dangerous, so as a front-line interpretive ranger, a big part of my job is warning visitors of the potential dangers of getting too close to a bear, or worse, startling a sow with cubs.

Educating visitors about bears begins when they enter the park. Signs at every entrance station warn that bears are dangerous. Visitors also are given information telling them how to avoid a bear confrontation and what to do if they encounter a bear up close and personal. In Glacier National Park's 97-year history we have had only ten

people killed by bears and average one "bear/human encounter" per year. Considering the fact that we have two million visitors a year our record is very good. Our goal, however, is to have no serious bear-human encounters. Therefore when visitors ask us about hiking in bear country we are, naturally, full of good advice. To have a safe experience in the wilderness of Glacier involves never hiking alone—the bigger the group, the better.

MARC MUENCH

Glacier National Park

We also tell our hikers that making a lot of noise is one of the best things they can do. When bears hear us coming they typically move off the trails. They may still be nearby, but we usually don't even know it. Bears generally don't want to have anything to do with us. They prefer to be left alone while they munch on berries, bulbs and insects.

This brings me to my story about a park interpreter (me) with many years of experience hiking Glacier's trails. I take 200 to 300 visitors on guided hikes every year. In addition to guided hikes, my friends and I hike close to 300 miles each summer. Many of our trips take us deep into bear country. We occasionally see a bear or two on a hillside, almost always at a good, safe distance.

One August morning, my assignment was to take visitors on a hike to Avalanche Lake. Avalanche Lake is a four-mile round trip during which we talk about the park's geology and its evolution into a wonderland of plants and animals. At the beginning of the trail (as with all of the park's trails) is a sign telling hikers they are entering a wilderness area with inherent dangers, including bears. I always emphasize the importance of people hiking in large groups (rule #1) and making lots of noise (rule #2) to ensure a safe trip, free from surprise wildlife encounters. The morning hike went well. Everyone had a great time and really seemed to connect with the park.

While driving back to the visitor center, I realized my entire afternoon was free to prepare for upcoming programs. I was scheduled to lead a 12-mile hike to a fire lookout the next week and could think of no better way to prepare than to take a test run on one of my favorite trails. After lunch I drove six miles to the Huckleberry Lookout Trailhead. I was so excited about the rest of my afternoon that I neglected to think much about the fact that this trail is called "Huckleberry" for a reason. It's full of huckleberries! Bears love huckleberries and migrate to this area in August and September because of all the ripe, juicy berries. Yikes, what was I thinking?!

As I started up the trail, there were two cars in the parking lot, so I assumed there were some hikers ahead of me. I disregarded the hundreds of warnings I had given visitors about not hiking alone and the need to make lots of noise. It was a great afternoon, not too cold and not too hot, with plenty of delicious huckleberries to munch on as I proceeded up the trail. Quickly and ever so QUIETLY I began to climb. It didn't even occur to me to be concerned about making noise. That was for the visitors to worry about! (At least I came prepared with bear spray.)

The first half mile of the Huckleberry Trail is level and the biggest challenge is getting past the masses of mosquitoes before climbing out of their wet, low-lying environment. As I climbed, I realized that I'd need to move at a fairly quick pace in order to make it to the fire lookout and back before dark. With my head down, I covered the next mile fast. After coming around a fairly sharp bend, I looked up and found myself staring at the biggest, blond-colored grizzly I had ever seen! It wasn't more than forty feet in front of me. All I could think of was "Oh Bill, what have you done?" Had I been noisy with lots of hiking companions, I probably wouldn't be in this mess. Instead, it was just me and this monster bear! I was dumbfounded and scared. I could beat myself up later for not doing the right things but first I had to figure out how to get out of this predicament in one piece.

To add to my nervousness, as soon as the bear saw me, it stood up on its hind legs and whuffed. Was it about to charge and neutralize me as a threat, or was it just curious? At that point I gathered my senses and decided that running would not be a good thing (at least at that moment). I pulled out my can of bear spray and unhooked the safety catch, standing as quietly as one could in such a circumstance.

Since the bear didn't charge or really look that aggressive it seemed the best thing to do was to slowly walk backward down the trail. The minute I moved, the bear began walking towards me. This was not the reaction I had hoped for, yet backing away and trying to appear non-threatening seemed like the best thing to do. I came to the sharp curve and moved around it. As I moved around the bend, I realized I could no longer see the bear. That meant that the bear couldn't see me either. With the bear out of sight, it was time to "get along." With my flat hat in one hand and bear spray in the other, I began to sprint. (Rule #3—if you ever see a bear, don't run!) By the time I reached my truck, I'm sure I set a world record.

As I stood by my truck, all I could do was laugh. If I had passed a group of hikers during my all-out sprint, I am sure they would have been laid out in laughter wondering what was going on with that ranger who passed them in such a hurry! I'd like to think the bear had a good laugh, too.

Using my radio I called our park bear management team so they could come up and safely bring out any hikers who were above the spot on the trail where I encountered that "monster bear." I drove back to our offices eager to tell of my good fortune in avoiding a really bad experience with a huge grizzly. I was proud of how well I handled the situation after I had been confronted by the most unpredictable of all bears. After telling my incredible tale, the radio crackled and the bear team member who went up the trail informed us that he spotted a blonde-colored black bear and that it probably didn't weigh more than 150 pounds. So much for my close encounter with a grizzly!

How fortunate I was to be able to chuckle at my experience on Huckleberry Trail that day. Others who have hiked quietly, without companions, or who have run away when confronting a wild animal have not always been so fortunate. Needless to say, I now follow my own advice: never hike alone, always check for news of recent bear sightings and, most importantly, make sure my hiking partners are good, loud singers!

Brutus the Bear

by Carol Jandrall

Black bears were causing increasing problems in the early 1990s at Whiskeytown National Recreation Area. They were getting into the trash at the campgrounds, picnic sites and dumpsters, causing a stir amongst rangers and park visitors alike. Some visitors were terrified that there were bears so close while others thought it was great to see them. They would even set up stakeouts at night to wait and watch the bears.

As a seasonal ranger in interpretation, I worked closely with the Resource Division and Law Enforcement Division in helping to educate park visitors about bear safety. This, of course, included the common sense rule that visitors shouldn't feed wild bears and also how to dispose of trash properly so as to not attract unwanted visitors in the middle of the night! During this period, our approach to dealing with bears in the campgrounds was to trap and relocate them to less populous areas of the park.

One of my early memories as a seasonal involves trying to capture one bear in particular; we called him Brutus. He was a large black bear, close to 400 pounds! Brutus was brown and looked like he had been around the block. Brutus had a consistent routine every evening. He would start at the Brandy Creek picnic area, knocking trash cans over and digging around for food in the garbage. He would then make his rounds at the marina,

 making his last stop at the campgrounds. Brutus was never in a hurry and was easily able to knock down the heavy cans with one swipe of his front paw.

Rangers used many tactics to scare bears away from the trash. We chased bears, yelled at them, used slingshots and even paintball guns. However, nothing we did seemed to deter Brutus. Once he was trapped and released far away from the campgrounds, but

returned a few days later, too wise to be trapped again. Our wildlife biologist came up with the idea of rigging a large can of pepper spray into a sophisticated system that would allow us to administer a targeted spray at Brutus while still remaining at a safe distance. The system consisted of a can of bear spray tied to a stake, with a long string attached to the trigger! We would set it up next to a big garbage can and stakeout the "crime scene" waiting for Brutus to arrive. We were sure that one good face full of pepper spray and Brutus would think twice about ever returning to the campgrounds.

One summer evening about 11 p.m., several other rangers and I set up the pepper spray trap. We were all quite pleased with our ingenious plan. I remember hearing Brutus across the lake making his rounds from can-to-can. As usual, he was unhurried. It seemed to take forever before he finally made it to where we were waiting. Our trash can had some tasty bear bait—it smelled like visitors had thrown away leftover fish and old cat food. (Bad smelling to us, but yummy for Brutus!) We had parked our ranger vehicle about 20 feet from the trap. The technologically advanced string system was all set up. Just in case Brutus got really mad, we had a ranger on top of the vehicle with a gun. Again, our hope was that one good face full of spray and we'd never see Brutus again.

Brutus slowly meandered past our covert location, making his way to his intended next meal. When he reached the trash can, he knocked it over with one easy swipe. The biologist pulled the string and the can burst into action, delivering a continuous spray of the hot pepper deterrent directly into Brutus's face. Brutus jumped back and shook his head. We were all watching very closely to see what he would do next. Much to our amazement, he simply returned his attention to the trash can and started enjoying his late-night snack, completely unfazed by the pepper spray. Simultaneously, the wind changed direction and the pepper spray wafted over to all of us. We started coughing and our eyes watered while Brutus happily continued eating away! So much for our ingenious plan.

Brutus continued to raid the cans that summer. Eventually fall and winter came and Brutus stopped coming around. The next summer, Brutus did not reappear and we'll never know what became of him. Eventually, bear proof trash cans and food storage lockers were installed, putting an end to bears getting into the trash. There are still plenty of bears in Whiskeytown and every time I pack a can of bear spray with my gear I chuckle and think of Brutus, who was surely smarter than the average bear (and ranger, too)!

LEE FOSTER

Whiskeytown National Recreational Area

Exploration & Adventure

The 1870s were a crucial period for national parks. John Muir, John Wesley Powell, Enos Mills, Clarence King, Nathaniel Langford and Thomas Moran (among many) were the pathfinders, the visionaries who inspired the creation of the parks. Today's park rangers continue in their footsteps, having new adventures and continuing to explore their beloved wilderness parks.

The national parks were born just after the Civil War, in a time of Indian wars, of unregulated early mining, logging, grazing and other rapacious uses of the land. Early explorers managed to see (and fight to preserve) the very best of our nation without the conveniences of four-wheel drive vehicles, jet airplanes, freeze-dried foods, lightweight waterproof fabrics—or salaries! They rode horses, trains or steamers and, for the most part, walked everywhere that cars take us today.

In the mid 19th century, when explorations were reaching their zenith, John Muir was the force behind the preservation of Yosemite National Park. The fight for Yosemite took 25 years of Muir's life. He also played an important role in exploring and preserving other areas, including Mammoth Cave, Glacier, Sequoia-Kings Canyon, Mount Rainier, Mount Shasta, Grand Canyon, Yellowstone and Glacier Bay.

John Wesley Powell was one of the first great explorers of the intermountain west region of North America. He was a scientist, able to survey and map the terrain, and an ethnologist able to communicate with Indians and learn about their culture. Without any previous maps or prior expedition notes to guide him, Powell descended the Colorado River from its headwaters on the Green River—2,000 miles into the great unknown. He had no knowledge of the navigability of the river. He didn't know if there were great waterfalls or rapids or whether there might be ways to escape the canyons if the expedition had to be aborted, how long the trip would take or what kind of boats would work best. Although Powell had lost an arm in the Civil War, he succeeded against all odds and emerged to inspire the nation with his accounts of what would become Dinosaur National Monument, Canyonlands and Grand Canyon National Parks and Lake Powel and Lake Mead National Recreation Areas.

Enos Mills, who made a home on Long's Peak and became known as the father of Rocky Mountain National Park, was an inveterate traveler. On a visit to San Francisco, he met John Muir, who encouraged his interests in the natural world, especially conservation, and urged him to write about his adventures in the wilderness. Enos took this advice and by the time he was 35, he had had visited every state and territory, and had traveled to Canada, Alaska and Mexico. Enos kept notes along the way, particularly about his main interests: zoology, botany, geology and meteorology.

Clarence King was the leader of the 40th parallel survey, a government mapping program that stretched across the west from California to Wyoming. He became the first director of the United States Geological Survey in 1879, contributing enormously to our understanding of the geology of the American west. He wrote Systematic Geology in 1878, and The Age of the Earth, in 1893, in which he estimated that the world was 24 million years old. He pioneered the use of contour lines, the precursor of topographic maps.

Nathaniel P. Langford, wrote magazine articles about Yellowstone, lectured extensively in the east and worked tirelessly to convince Congress to set aside the land for the public. He was responsible for a government expedition in 1871 that explored the area and he worked on the legislation that resulted in the establishment of the park in 1872, well prior to the creation of the National Park Service in 1916. He took charge of Yellowstone during its first five years and not only wasn't paid, but had to pay all his own expenses as well. He had no assistants and little authority, and really had to struggle to protect the park. He had explored much of Yellowstone and documented what he found, but many who read his accounts of geysers, hot springs and other wonders found them very difficult to believe.

Thomas Moran was an immigrant who had settled in New York and worked as an artist. He was a talented illustrator and became one of the premier painters of American landscapes. His paintings had tremendous influence on western tourism and on the members of Congress who set aside vast areas of the west as national parks. Stephen Mather, the first director of the National Park Service, said that Moran, "more than any other artist has made us acquainted with the Great West..." The incredibly beautiful images that he created from his travels to Yellowstone, the Grand Canyon, Yosemite Valley and other wild places earned Moran the nickname "Father of the National Park System," a title that history also bestowed on a number of his fellow explorers who were instrumental in establishing the National Park Service.

Today's rangers have big shoes to fill and big dreams to live. There are still many adventures to be sure—for both rangers and visitors—and what better settings then the wilderness areas protected within our national parks. Working together, we can only hope to fulfill the goals and expectations of the great explorers who first envisioned "America's best idea"—our national parks.

Forty-Five Days in the Alaskan Wilderness

by Daryl Miller

Five hours after breaking camp, Mark and I were traveling in darkness. The winter days were very short and very cold. Eighty miles and seven days from the warmth of Talkeetna, we settled into the discomfort that's bound to accompany a 350-mile winter ski patrol around the wild perimeter of Mount McKinley and Mount Foraker. Wind off the frozen Chulitna River scoured our exposed skin. We struggled with our packs and snow pigs—the heavy sleds that carried our assortment of gear. The pain was bearable, but there were 270 miles of Denali wilderness left and an array of obstacles to overcome.

The eighth day was nice. The wind had relented a bit and I could feel my nose for the first time in a week. Mark's tiny, clip-on thermometer indicated a relatively balmy 15 degrees below zero as we entered the river's first major canyon complex.

Granite walls blocked the sun, creating a strange shadowy world. The snow was deep and soft. Trail-breaking was slow and laborious. This was far different than standing in the Talkeetna ranger station sliding a finger along frozen rivers on the big wall map or flying over the route in an airplane. My thoughts went back to that warm comfortable place, but my daydream ended quickly with the loud crack beneath my skis and the heaving of the unstable shelf ice. As our route approached a narrow section of river channel, I noticed several deep, open leads. Rushing water echoed violently against towering cliff walls.

Then, the worst happened. A snowy trapdoor gave way beneath my skis, and I plunged into the river. The current sucked me downstream beneath the ice. Panic filled my chest. I struggled to hook my arms over the wafer-thin edge of ice circling the black hole. The swift current knocked me off balance. The pig teetered

MARC MUENCH

Denali National Park and Preserve

on the edge, ready to fall. I knew that if the sled went in, the extra drag would pull me under and it would be all over. I yelled for Mark, but wasn't sure if he could hear or see me. My breathing turned ragged in the freezing water.

Finally, I heard Mark answer, but I couldn't understand the words. Then I saw him about 25 feet away. He pulled a throw bag—a floatable, water rescue device attached to a rope—from his sled. He tossed it to me, but I couldn't reach it. The tangled, frozen wad of rope fell ten feet short. Mark reeled it back and threw it again.

That time it hit me. I clutched the rope—and safety—and Mark quickly pulled me from the hole. I was focused on the danger of freezing to death while Mark pulled out a camera and took a picture. He smiled and said it would be a shame not to document the event.

A giant bonfire would have been great, but there was no wood. I took off my wet clothes, slipped into dry polypropylene and downed the hot tea that Mark had quickly prepared on our camp stove. He shook the ice out of my frozen but still functional wind suit while I dumped the water out of my "bunny boots"—rubber boots with thick layers of wool insulation—and pulled them back on over dry socks. Then we were off again.

By day 17, we were approaching Gunsight Pass, where we roped up. Some of the crevasse bridges in the lower icefall appeared questionable. The pass looked climbable, but with heavy packs, bunny boots and the pigs, it was almost certain to be an exercise in high anxiety. When that climb was finally behind us, we descended onto Peter's Glacier, only to wallow in waist-deep snow. It took us three days to reach our second cache at the head of the Muddy River north of the Alaska Range.

On the coldest day of the trip—Mark's thermometer fell to minus 40 degrees—we approached our third food cache. This cache had been left under a single-flagged spruce tree. Looking across the vast taiga near the Swift Fork, we noticed with dismay that all the spruce trees looked alike. So did the desolate hills and barren ice lakes. I argued for a lone spruce tree about a quarter mile away, but Mark held out for a tree three miles away. (Good thing, because he was right!)

As a full moon rose, we trudged through the extreme cold to the tree and then struggled to pitch the tent, which had frozen into a cylinder of ice after we splashed through Somber Creek. It was a stiff and icy shrine when we finally got it up. After brewing hot soup, we collapsed into our lumpy, frozen sleeping bags.

Early the next morning, we neared the ridge separating us from the Chedotlothna Glacier. We had our eyes on a spot we dubbed "Nomad Pass," where we could cross back to the south side of the Alaska Range. The weather was cold and felt colder because of a gusty, nasty wind blowing out of the north. We climbed down several rope lengths into a crevasse and to the edge of a 30-foot-deep snow bridge. We probed it for stability, then chipped a platform for the tent, thinking we'd fare better there than on the exposed, unstable snow above.

The next morning, Mark led us out of the crevasse and up a long crack in the glacial ice, chopping belay platforms as he went. Mark climbed a rope length on belay, then I followed, leaving our sleds tied to the end. Together, we pulled the pigs up to each belay platform.

The headwall was a constant 50 degrees, sometimes increasing to 60 degrees. We tried to stay near a band of rock along one side because of avalanche danger. Mark chopped 13 platforms in the course of the day. At each, we labored to haul up the 150-pound pigs. The tiny thermometer said it was minus 30. By dark, we topped out in worsening weather. The wind was blowing so hard that it was difficult to breathe. We knew that we couldn't survive that for long. There was no choice but to rappel toward the Yentna Glacier.

Hacking through a thick coat of ice, we prepared a rock to hold the rope for the descent, set so we could pull the rope down at the end. The rappel into the darkness was slow and punishing in the screaming wind. Finally, we located an ice ledge and chopped a place for the tent. We tied it with rope to hold it in place.

The night passed with little sleep. Morning light helped us to push on. The wind-whipped snow howled and visibility was zero. Traveling unknown ground with no landmarks, we descended by compass through a crevassed maze, blindly feeling for solid footing in hurricane-force wind that smashed us to the ground over and over. We resorted to crawling to a huge boulder that provided our only shelter from the wind. Working feverishly, we chopped another tent platform. Ice screws and carabineers held down the tent. The climbing rope was tied over it like a giant fish net, in the hope that it would keep the nylon from ripping apart.

By morning, we just wanted off the glacier. We began a six-mile trek downslope to the "Trench," a deep, glacial river laced with crevasses near the juncture of the Yentna and Lacuna Glaciers. At first glance, the crossing appeared rather easy, but it took two full days of miserable travel to cover the next two miles. Many times we crossed broken sections of ice laced with house-sized blocks formed by intersecting crevasses. The pigs sometimes hung eagerly below us, inviting a quick trip down. On day 39, we spent the night at the bottom of the trench, shivering after eating the last cup of instant mashed potatoes. Our food supply had run short and it was 20 tough miles to the next cache. The next day, we climbed out of the trench, over the Ramparts Range and, at last, began the descent of the familiar Kahiltna Glacier.

By day 42 we found ourselves lying in the tent not wanting to move. We drank lots of water before setting out and ate snow most of the day and, while well hydrated, we were low on energy. Our last push took us up Cache Creek, only a few miles short of the precious cache on Spruce Creek. Languishing in the tent, dreaming of food, we heard snowmobiles in the distance. Human contact appeared imminent for the first time in more than a month.

Two days and 30 miles later, we crossed the not-so-frozen Chulitna and walked down Talkeetna's main street, returning home. We'd been on the trail for 45 days and traveled 350 miles. I'd lost 25 pounds. Most surprisingly, we'd returned better friends than when we left. The rest of our experience—the solitude and the fear, the joy and the agony, the hardships and the pleasures—is all but impossible to explain. We'll cherish it forever.

Where Does That Hole Go?

by Jim Pisarowicz

"Oh, Ranger, where does that hole go?" asked an inquisitive ten-year-old girl on a tour I was leading one day. This is one of the most common questions I hear at Wind Cave National Park, one of the longest and most complex caves in the world.

I answer, "That hole could lead you into over 100 miles of known cave. In fact, if you knew your way, it could take you all the way to the bottom, where you would find a series of hidden underground lakes."

"Have you been there?" she asked, wide-eyed with excitement.

I smiled and began my story...

I work at Wind Cave because I am a caver, a person who explores and studies caves. I have been in over 5,000 caves around the world. I'm often asked to name my favorite.

"Whichever one I'm in at the moment is my favorite," I always say, "and right now that's Wind Cave." It's not that I'm avoiding the question. As a caver, my favorites are the ones still being explored, and Wind Cave still has many secrets left to discover. So far, over 123 miles of passages have been recorded, which makes it the 4th longest cave in the world. (The longest is Mammoth Cave, which can be found in another wonderful national park in the Green River valley of southcentral Kentucky.)

In the early 1970s, Windy City Grotto, a caving club from Chicago, discovered a lake at the bottom of the cave. They named it Windy City Lake after their club. At 500 feet below the surface, it's the lowest known point in Wind Cave. With much difficulty, the club members carried an inflatable boat down to the bottom of the cave so that they could cross the lake. In their report they noted that they had checked all the passageways (called "leads")

out of the room across Windy City Lake and found them all to be dead ends.

Finding all the lead passageways in Wind Cave has been difficult because the cave is different than most caves that form in limestone. Limestone has many cracks and fissures, so when water, which is slightly acidic, gets into the cracks, it very slowly dissolves the limestone. When caves form in this way, they tend to have main channels that flow like a river. Wind Cave is different. Although it formed in limestone that was dissolved by acid-charged groundwater, the water in Wind Cave filled all the cracks and slowly dissolved the limestone, leaving open cave rooms. Wind Cave is not like an underground river, but more like a gigantic sponge, with passageways going in every direction.

Because of the sponge-like nature of the cave, it is nearly impossible to check out all the passageways. Knowing this, I planned a trip in 1986 to the far side of Windy City Lake, a place where no one had been for over 14 years. I was accompanied by Bob, another caver who also worked at the park.

A trip to the bottom of Wind Cave is long and grueling. When we filled out the trip permit, we indicated that we expected to be in the cave for 24 hours. The permits are important because they allow the park to monitor cave travel. They're also important for cavers because they indicate the route being taken into the cave and the amount of time expected for the trip. If we did not check in after 24 hours, the park would send a search party to look for us along our proposed travel route.

Both Bob and I carried our usual assortment of equipment, including water, food, garbage bags, maps and survey apparatus (compass, inclinometer, notebook) in our packs. We also each carried two lights, in addition to helmet lamps and wetsuits for the swim across the lakes, plus bottles for water samples. The samples are used by researchers studying the aquifer.

Both of us were dressed in jeans, old shirts and boots, with knee and elbow pads. Using our knowledge of the cave and occasionally consulting our maps, we reached the shore of Windy City Lake in about two hours. Our bodies were bruised from crawling on hands and knees through long stretches of the cave. Since leaving the visitor tour path, we were rarely able to stand or walk on flat ground. Occasionally we had to get down on our bellies and squirm through passages only eight to ten inches high. In other places we had to climb up and down narrow fissures up to 75-feet tall. As I used my flashlight to scan the clear blue water of Windy City Lake, I just wanted to rest and

MARC MUENCH

Wind Cave National Park

catch my breath for a couple of minutes.

Finally I reached into my pack and pulled out my wetsuit. Soon, both Bob and I were suited up. We packed our gear and clothes in triple trash bags and headed for the opposite shore. I shivered when I stepped into the lake. The water between my wetsuit and skin felt cold. The temperature in Wind Cave tends to run about 53° F, but the lake water is slightly warmer, around 55° F. This is because the groundwater is warmed by geothermal heat. Eleven miles south of the park at the town of Hot Springs, the water comes out of the ground at 87° F.

The swim across the lake was about 100 yards and the trash bags kept everything pretty dry. Bob and I stripped off our wetsuits and changed back into dry clothes. I took out my copy of the Windy City Grotto survey notes and began checking them against the passages we saw in the room. I suggested that Bob check out every hole on the left side of the room while I checked out every hole on the right side. Just as the notes indicated, lead after lead went nowhere, until I happened to look up at the ceiling. There, right above me, was a narrow slot. I pulled myself up into the passage and before long I was looking down across another lake.

"Boy," I thought to myself, "I better go back and get Bob."

When I emerged from the ceiling, I startled Bob. Like the cavers 14 years earlier, he had not seen the lead in the ceiling.

"Bob!" I yelled, "I found another lake!"

"But I thought this was the end of the cave," Bob replied.

"It's not!" I said. "Come on, get out the survey gear and let's start mapping this new section."

We named the new lake "Lake Land." After crossing it and climbing up through another hole, we found a second lake we named "Evans Plunge," after the hot spring in the town of Hot Springs.

After a downward climb we found a third, even larger lake, and then a huge passage. The ceilings were 40 to 50 feet high and the passage was 60 to 70 feet wide. We called this passage the "Mammoths' Backbone," and a fourth lake off of to the side we dubbed the "Inner Sea."

Passages went off in all directions. Bob found yet another lake that he called the "Lovely Little Lake." Finally, we had to begin the long trip back up to the surface in order to get out in time to check in. We turned around in a passage 50 feet wide and 30 feet high.

On the way back we paused at the largest lake discovered earlier that day. It took me a few minutes to figure out how to climb back up. While I was looking over the climb, Bob suggested that since we had not yet named that lake, we should name it after ourselves... "Jim-Bobs Plunge."

Bob and I returned to that section of Wind Cave many times and others followed. We eventually mapped more than a mile of the passage.

By the end of 1986 Wind Cave's explored length was 48 miles, which made it the 7th longest cave in the world. Twenty years later, by the end of 2006, the explored length was almost 123 miles, the world's 4th longest explored cave. There is no end in sight.

I consider myself part of a long line of explorers of Wind Cave. The cave's first real explorer, Alvin McDonald, started exploring Wind Cave in 1890. He wrote in his diary on January 23, 1891: "Have given up the idea of finding the end of Wind Cave..." Over a hundred years later I could not agree more! I'm sure future explorers of Wind Cave will also agree with Alvin. I have met many of them already. They show up on my tours everyday in Wind Cave and say:

"Oh Ranger, where does that hole go?"

Reliving the Stormy Past

by Jon Preston

The mountains seem to rise from the edge of the water, on both sides, in steep ascent to the line of perpetual snow, as though nature had designed to shut up this spot for her safe retreat forever.

Territorial Governor Eugene Semple, Seattle Press, July 16, 1890

The water was moving fast, banking off logjams and flooding countless side channels. It looked impossible to ford. The worst August storm in the recorded history of the Olympic Mountains had turned the Elwha River from postcard serenity to ferocious and deadly. Only three miles beyond the opposite bank and some 1,500 feet higher, the Low Divide Ranger Station would offer a place to dry out and warm up. I was accompanying a group of notable travel and outdoor writers, complete with packer and gourmet chef, on a 52-mile wilderness trek across Olympic National Park.

Now, deep in the heart of the mountains and after a night of torrential rain, many were drenched, cold and starting to show early signs of exposure. A lack of subcutaneous body fat may make a person look good in the city, but here, soaked to the skin, the skinny folk were in trouble. While I was considering our alternatives, the group's chef walked right into the raging torrent. Using his lengthy staff for support and loaded with suicidal bravado, he broke the water like a ship in a stormy sea. To my horror he moved through the fast-moving river with water nearly to his waist. Only by sheer luck did he make it across.

Organized by the local tourism bureau and billed as a reenactment of the original 1889 Seattle Press Expedition, this was supposed to be a media junket... literally a walk in the park. Now it was a test of survival uncomfortably similar to the experiences

MARC MUENCH

Olympic National Park

of the original expedition some 110 years before.

In the late 1800s the Olympic Mountains, although known to American Indians for thousands of years, remained one of the last vestiges of the continental United States that settlers had not explored. A reporter for the fledgling Seattle newspaper, the Seattle Press, wrote, "Washington has her great unknown land like the interior of Africa." And the territorial governor reported to Congress "...men have gone all around this section as bush men go all around a jungle in which a man eating tiger is concealed, but the interior is incognito."

Funded by the Seattle Press in 1889, the expedition wanted to discover what wonders lay beyond the Olympic's periphery. To claim that they were the first expedition to cross the mountains, they plunged head-on into the unknown interior of the Olympic Peninsula in a bitterly cold December. Consisting of five men, four dogs, two mules and 1500 pounds of supplies, the expedition suffered many tribulations. Naming peaks as they traversed the rugged territory, they exited "weary and footsore" in May. The Seattle Press subsequently printed a detailed account of their exploits for a curious public.

The original exploration took place during the snowy winter of 1889-1890 and the reenactment was in late August, statistically a time of sunshine and warm weather in the Olympic Mountains. "So much for statistical probability," I thought to myself while pondering our predicament.

There was no way I could send the rest of the group across the torrent, so I searched upstream for a better point to cross. After some perseverance and wading through a number of swollen flood channels, I found a log that spanned the bulk of the river, but it wasn't going to be easy to cross. The log was wet, narrow and bouncy, and each member of the group would be forced to slip off the end and drop into the river for a few steps before they could reach the other side. The chef redeemed himself by helping me get everyone safely across and I breathed a deep sigh of relief. I notified the rangers at Low Divide not to send anyone down this way until the rain had stopped and the water had receded. In January of 1890, after the press expedition ferried their supply-filled boat through Elwha rapids, one member noted "As we managed to get out of the freezing water the air changed our garments to ice in a moment... all of us were livid blue for some time after it was over..."

The Low Divide was still 1,500 feet above us, and to get there we had to hike along a narrow trail that had been blasted out by the Civilian Conservation Corps. I sent the wet travelers up two-by-two and brought up the rear. About halfway up, a powerful waterfall was dumping directly onto the narrow trail and one of the stronger members of the group waited on the other side to offer assistance. Reaching through, I grabbed his hand and was yanked through the cascade. In the process, the pounding water ripped the hood off my parka and the cold water streamed down my back. Shivering and miserable, my concern about the other members of the group intensified.

The smoke curling out of the ranger station chimney was a welcome sight! We had all made it and the rangers let our entire group into the station. It was packed like a subway car. The wood stove cranked out heat and made the interior feel a bit like a sauna. The whole place reeked of wet wool socks that had been worn for way too many days, but no one minded. I could see that each person had grown a bit. The accomplishment of having overcome difficulty together created a family out of a group of independent-minded individuals.

We still had quite a distance to hike before we would arrive home again, but I relaxed a little and enjoyed the moment. The rain continued to fall unabated for the next 36 hours. Thankfully, all the gear arrived with the packers on the backs of some very sodden mules. After we got the tents set up outside, we began to try to dry out the sleeping bags. The group wore out their welcome at the ranger station pretty quickly and we reluctantly returned to our campsite. Warm drink, good food and lots of storytelling passed the time until we departed two days later.

> *So we sat around the fire and kept the frying pans going and drank the grease as fast as we could fry it out.*
>
> Captain Charles Barnes, Press Expedition Journal, May 5th, 1890

A clear morning greeted us for the 16-mile hike down the Quinault valley and our return to civilization. Quite a bit of fanfare greeted us at Quinault Lodge. That evening a huge reception was held in our honor. I attended the gala, even though a hot shower and clean clothes were all I really wanted. Our group had bonded through our shared experience, enjoying the camaraderie that comes from overcoming adversity together. I also gained a deeper appreciation of what those early explorers had to endure, and know that we shared the universal lessons that span the breadth of human experience.

Letters from the Lewis and Clark Trail

by Nancy Marie Hoppe

"No last minute thoughts from this end. I'm just happy that you are joining us. I'll see you at the airport..." These were the words of my detail supervisor as I prepared to meet his team in Boise, Idaho, to start a temporary assignment. Never one to venture far from Missouri or Illinois, I was embarking on the adventure of a lifetime, becoming a part of the only traveling national park in the history of the National Park Service. Corps of Discovery II: 200 Years to the Future would retrace the steps of Lewis and Clark. Before this trip, I had only imagined the travels of these historical figures, as I walked the corridors of the Museum of Westward Expansion beneath the Gateway Arch in St. Louis at my home park, Jefferson National Expansion Memorial. Much like the famous explorers who came before me, I documented my thoughts and feelings along the way. My letters reveal the heart of a woman who, in almost three decades of service, has been challenged and changed. I know now that I have two families. The letters from my time on the Lewis and Clark trail provide a window to a special time with my National Park Service family.

Missoula, Montana
June 23, 2006

A fellow traveler taught me how to smell the river water for salmon and how to tell if trees were burned in fires years ago or damaged in avalanches. We collected a few small rocks from the Clearwater River. We drove over the Bitterroots, the Continental Divide and the Lolo Trail. There were abundant evergreen trees for miles. I imagined how beautiful they must look in winter and what convulsions I would go through if I

MARC MUENCH

Jefferson National Expansion Memorial

had to drive in ice and snow up this pass!

Lincoln, Montana
June 28, 2006

Standing on the Fort Missoula parade ground in Missoula, Montana, I realized that no matter which direction I looked, I was surrounded by beautiful mountains.

Lincoln, Montana
July 3, 2006

Coworkers showed me where deer had rubbed the trees, leaving marks. They also showed me where porcupines had eaten bark way up high in the pine trees. I didn't know that porcupines even got off the ground! We even smelled tree bark that reminded me of maple syrup.

Cut Bank, Montana
July 4, 2006

The drive to Cut Bank was befitting an Independence Day. I cried when I heard Phil Driscoll's "America" and other patriotic songs on the radio. To think that I was crossing my country on July 4th, representing the National Park Service, seeing land I had never seen before, hearing songs about this land I love. What an adventure! I wonder if Lewis and Clark shared similar feelings 200 years ago.

I went to a small-town fireworks display. It didn't compare to the elaborate fireworks under the Gateway Arch but it was still wonderful. I thought about how hard the staff back home must have worked that day, with the heat and crowds and so many long hours. I thought about my kids and the times we'd watch the fireworks at the Arch and then run to our car to beat the crowd out of the parking lot.

Glacier National Park
July 10, 2006

Today, I am one very sore Corps II member. Maybe this is why Lewis and Clark took 100 gallons of whiskey with them! My soreness was caused by activities yesterday in AWESOME Glacier National Park. It was well worth the body slamming. I thought the trail to Hidden Lake in alpine tundra was a wildflower walk, and it started that way, but then wooden planks and steps appeared for climbing up around a mountain low spot called a "saddle." At the bottom of trail, I saw snow in the distance. Soon I was walking in it! It took me almost two hours to walk a mile. I fell a lot. At one point the mountain just seemed to fall away at a 90-degree angle. It was hard to believe the drop, which appeared to be three times the height of the Arch, my frame of reference. I really didn't want to go down there. I made it to Hidden Lake, where there was the most beautiful scene: water, exposed rock, evergreen trees, wildflowers and animals. A family of mountain goats walked right in front of me and bighorn sheep looked on from a nearby mountain ledge.

Then the return trip! Well, I was terrified. But at the most dangerous point a ranger, stationed there for obvious reasons, caught me so I wouldn't take a monumental trip down the slope. With the aid of coworkers, and shaking like a leaf, I crawled sideways until I felt I could walk again. The beautiful waterfalls helped to distract me as I struggled along the slippery path. I learned about Krumholtz trees—with stunted, flaglike tops due to strong wind and permafrost—and Yarrow plants, which smelled like the ointment used for aching muscles. (I secretly wished I had a gallon of the stuff, as I knew I'd be aching after this long trek!) I also learned a great way to identify lodgepole pine trees by their L-shaped pine needles.

Billings, Montana
July 29 2006

I was so looking forward to see Pompey's Pillar, one of the most famous sandstone buttes in America. Clark named the pillar in honor of Sacagawea's son, Jean Baptiste Charbonneau, who he had nicknamed "Pomp." It holds the only remaining physical evidence of the expedition. On July 25, 1806, Captain William Clark carved his name on the face of the giant rock on his way back through the Yellowstone Valley. I'd only seen it before in pictures. Walking up the steps, I met park archivist, Jennifer and her husband Charley, who is a descendant of William Clark. How exciting for me to have my picture taken between those two with the famous signature behind us!

On the weekend, I rented a car and a cabin at Old Faithful Lodge in Yellowstone National Park. Several times while driving through Yellowstone, I began to cry so hard that I had to pull over. Everything was so beautiful that I couldn't believe I was actually there! Other times, I laughed out loud, thanking God for the chance to travel, for this assignment, and for the people who allowed me to go. I had the time of my life raising and home-schooling my three daughters. On this detail, I had the second time of my life. I saw so much beauty: hot springs, mud volcanoes, steaming geysers, fumaroles, water falls, fishermen, ospreys, a jack rabbit, elk and buffalo galore. The buffalo caused traffic jams! They strolled down the middle of the road with a line of cars following slowly behind them. I walked the maze of boardwalks around Old Faithful for hours. It was my favorite activity.

Driving through the park, I thought about why we have a National Park Service and why this area was chosen to be the first park. America is so big and beautiful. I hope my children and their families get to go to Yellowstone. I knew I'd really hate to leave the amazing place and hoped visitors felt the same way when leaving all of our national parks, especially mine in St. Louis. Charles Ross, the man who originally hired me to work for the National Park Service in 1972, died while I was on this assignment. I felt like Yellowstone completed a circle in my life somehow, as I'd heard discussed in American Indian culture.

New Town, North Dakota
August 16, 2006

Before I left Miles City, I met the grandson of western photographer Christian Barthelmess. As I toured his Range Riders Museum, the senior volunteers showed me pictures and personal belongings of their relatives. They touched my heart with memories of long-gone people and objects that were now museum relics. These treasures were displayed in rooms baking in the heat, with no security cameras and within easy reach. Where would these memories be if it weren't for the care of these volunteers and their love of keeping and sharing lives long past?

St. Louis, Missouri
October 9, 2006

I was so fearful at the beginning of the assignment that I considered telling my boss that I couldn't do it. I confess that, if I had seen the Corps II team in action, I would never have applied. The amount of heavy lifting alone would have scared me away. You see, I have polio. Surely my body wasn't equipped for the physical demands of the job. The Corps II team allowed me to lift what I could and they lifted the rest. The amazing

National Park Service! Not only does it protect our parks for all visitors to enjoy, but it allows me, a woman with a physical handicap, to have this wonderful job!

At the headwaters of the Missouri, Lewis said that Hugh McNeal "had exultingly stood with a foot on each side of this little rivulet and thanked his god that he had lived to bestride the mighty and heretofore deemed endless Missouri..." Being here, on this journey, gives me a sense of what Hugh must have felt over two centuries ago. How amazing it must have been to be there and hear his stories. I would have loved to share with him how blessed I feel to have followed in his footsteps. The Bible says, "He loads us down daily with blessings." This expedition was one of God's special gifts to me.

Now when I rove around the Museum of Westward Expansion under the Arch, I no longer need to look at the 33 giant murals that line the walls to appreciate the excitement and adventure that Lewis and Clark must have felt. No, now all I have to do is close my eyes and remember the trip I made with my family of fellow rangers on the Corps of Discovery II.

The Wild South Coast

by Don Follows

The land "don't care" if you live or die,
Chase bald eagles across the sky,
Or greet all dangers eye to eye.
The land won't care how hard you try!
But it's up to you if you live or die!

In 1975, my first assignment as a National Park Service ranger took me to the Alaskan wilderness with two primary objectives:

1. Become an expert on the natural resources and wildlife of the Harding Icefield and surrounding coastal region.
2. Do everything possible to develop a proposal to incorporate this area into the National Park System.

I embarked on an adventure to the Kenai Peninsula as a member of the Alaska Task Force. It was an ambitious task for a new ranger, but one I accepted with great optimism. I would be investigating two mysterious lakes left behind by the meltdown of a former tidewater glacier—a place with no geographic delineation, not to be found on any map!

Wedged between the Harding Icefield and the Gulf of Alaska, this isolated coast had witnessed few visits by modern humans. For millennia, the region had been covered in glacial sheets of ice and snow, dominated by the mile-high Harding Icefield. Only a few fishermen had ever sailed past the remote wave-battered cliffs, islands and sea stacks, which would later be called "Kenai

MARC MUENCH

Kenai Fjords National Park

Fjords." My field investigations and reports were the first comprehensive evaluations of the coastal region's geology, wildlife and intrinsic resource values.

During the hour-long flight to the site, my pilot Ralph and I marveled at the beauty of thousand-foot waterfalls, cascading down mountain snowfields into dark seas and rocky shoals. We could see small bands of mountain goats grazing on green tundra carpets, while bald eagles soared below us in search of prey. As we looked across the endless Gulf of Alaska, Ralph reminded me that somewhere in that broad expanse were the Hawaiian Islands!

After circling the area, I directed Ralph to land in the bay near the mouth of a stream. After a perfect water landing on the plane's pontoons, he cut the engine and we glided into the shallows. The tide was up. The sea was flat. It was a perfect day. I grabbed my backpack and quickly waded through the cold ocean to the flat, sandy beach. Ralph would pick me up here the following afternoon for my return flight to headquarters in Anchorage. It seemed safe to "go it alone" for just one day.

We had no radio communication in those days. Except for a handshake and kind-worded reminder to the pilot not to forget them, rangers were on their own. "Never sign the invoice until the plane returns," was the standard joke for task force members.

It was late in the day when Ralph dropped me onto the beach and fired up the Cessna engine for his return flight. The floatplane opened its throttle and roared across the calm ocean waters. Gaining air speed, it lifted up and headed into the Gulf of Alaska. The heavy drone of the plane's engine was soon replaced by waves gently lapping on the beach. I watched the plane became smaller and smaller, until it was swallowed into the immensity of the Alaskan landscape.

Isolated and confident in my seaside solitude, I pitched my mountain tent, gathered driftwood for the evening fire and caught some Dolly Varden trout for dinner. No sense wasting my meager rations if an easy meal of fish was available. I took time to explore the shoreline and observe the plants and animals whose home I would now be sharing. The long days under the midnight sun could not be wasted. Resource familiarity was not only of scientific interest, but sound necessity. I'd learned growing up in the Rocky Mountains as a subsistence hunter and angler that a strong knowledge of one's immediate surroundings could mean the difference between life and death, should something go wrong in the wilderness.

As the midnight sun sank below the Kenai Mountains to the northwest, my eyes scanned across the quiet lagoon where several sea otters were hauled up on the beach a hundred yards from camp. A small black bear patrolled the far edge of the swelling tide line. A friendly porcupine wandered past me and disappeared into the dark spruce forest, all potential food if need be! As the embers of my campfire faded, I pondered the fact that the spot where I now camped had been—until quite recently in geological terms—covered by a mile-high sheet of glacial ice for over 60,000 years!

The early morning sun warmed my dew-soaked tent and I awakened to the sweet smell of ocean mist. I heard the excited cries of a hundred gulls swooping down on the bay like a white blizzard. A large cluster of herring was concentrated close to the surface. My objective for the day was to follow the small stream leading to the glacial lake we had seen in the over flight in order to study the salmon habitat. My travels were interrupted by white, volcanic ash freshly deposited from the eruption of Mt. Augustine. The ash dropped onto my hat and shoulders from the spruce branches above. Each stride towards the hidden lake stirred up the fine dust.

I could not see salmon in the stream. After years of maturing at sea, salmon return to their freshwater birth streams to spawn and die. Through some unknown navigational system, they find their way back to where they were hatched. Had there been enough time since the glacier meltdown for the new lake and stream to attract salmon populations? Unaltered by humans, the lake might provide scientists clues as to how the first salmon locate and populate new lakes formed after glacier retreat. The cycle had to start somewhere!

By noon of the first day, sunshine had vanished as dark clouds rolled down from the Harding Icefield. Merging with a warmer air system somewhere in the Gulf of Alaska, skies turned black and ominous. Sudden collisions of warm and cold air erupted over my head, dumping heavy rain showers on land and sea. I hurried back to my tent, tightened down the pegs and crawled inside to escape the lashing winds now sweeping in from the sea.

During the next days and nights, rain, hail and sleet, driven by violent winds, confined me within the bone-chilling cold of my small tent. Winds gusted to more than fifty miles an hour, as sheets of endless rain raced horizontally across my open campsite. My tent shuddered under heavy and frequent wind blasts. Behind me in the forest, the storm's onset blew volcanic ash into blinding white clouds of dust. Rain soon turned volcanic ash into a slimy, muddy paste that dripped from the trees. For a while, the nearby creek flowed like mushroom soup. It was an endless storm. I knew the plane could not return in these conditions.

In short order, my land of serenity had become a cold, wet and dark encounter with weather, which only time and patience could overcome. Day after day, night after night, the summer storm would not release its furious grip. Trying to cook what little food I had on my gas stove was difficult. Wind surges continued to blast the tent sides and flaps, knocking my backpack stove off its stand near the entrance. It had been nearly three days since I had a solid meal. I stayed inside and inactive. I read my book, slept, drank water and slept again. Could I stay a week if need be?

Temperatures dropped radically. I tried to stay inside my tent and sleeping bag to conserve energy and fend off hypothermia. Wind gusts continued to torture my exposed shelter. One strong blast ripped the rain fly off one corner of the tent. To get out of the tent and re-secure the flapping line exposed me to the cold, pelting rain. Back inside my sleeping bag, my body began to shiver uncontrollably. My basic food had been exhausted by the end of the second day. How long it would take for my pickup was unknown. My mind wandered to the documented cases in which pilots forgot where they dropped off their clients. I worried about my wife who thought I'd be returning the next day. I'd never failed to return as planned from past field trips, but Alaska was different from my previous adventures in Yellowstone and the red rock canyons of Utah.

By noon on the fifth day, the rain and wind had stopped. I crawled out of my rain-soaked shelter and took a long walk to exercise my cramping legs. My "natural" food sources were still living nearby. Having been raised in the west on wild game and fish, I felt no conflict in taking wildlife to sustain human life in times of critical need. But my firewood was still soaked and I preferred not to eat raw meat!

Suddenly, I heard the drone of an airplane high above me. A small spot had cleared in the dark sky. Through it dropped the Cessna 172. It was Ralph! I waved, ran back to the campsite, gathered up my gear, dropped the tent and packed it. I was both anxious and ready to leave camp when Ralph cut the plane's engine and pointed the prop toward shore.

While it wasn't the trip I had expected, I did have time to find a glacial lake jammed with spawning salmon. But when did salmon first find this stream and spawning lake so soon after glaciers released their tenuous hold? I hoped that future scientists might study this outdoor museum for clues into the Pacific salmon life cycle and their sudden adaptation to new glacial landscapes. For now, many of my questions remained unanswered.

On the long flight home, I reflected on the vast, dangerous and indifferent Alaskan landscape. Then, ready to move on, thoughts of a nice hot meal and a warm bed began to fill my head.

Wild Manhattan!

by C.W. Buchholtz

It took me a week or two to recover from a recent trip to New York City. On returning home, the highlight of my therapy was a long walk in the woods.

While not a big city person, I'd been to the Big Apple before, but only a couple of times and most recently over a decade ago. Visiting the urban east always comes as a shock to my western state of mind. New York, I'm certain, is the apex of sophistication and urbanism. But it is a very long way, physically if not intellectually, from the forests and valleys of Rocky Mountain National Park.

When I started my early winter stroll, memories of a frenzied taxi ride were as fresh in my mind as the wind was raw. Clouds loomed along the Continental Divide, blocking my view of the mountains, just as towers of concrete had covered the midtown horizon.

Forsaking cars (and cabs) and trails (too manufactured), I set out to climb a forested ridge. The noise of civilization drifted away. A breeze touching the tops of ponderosa pines gave the woods a murmuring voice. I was "shaking off the rust of civilization," as naturalist John Muir might say.

During the first hour of walking, I simply enjoyed being alone. In the woods, there was no waiting in line. There were no security checks. There were no worries about needing directions or wondering where I was going. I was home.

Friends always warn me about the hazards of hiking alone. I'm aware of the dangers, take many precautions and feel I have little to fear. Once, when I was working as a ranger, I was standing near my patrol car at Logan Pass in Glacier National Park. A small red car bearing Massachusetts plates and two young women pulled up beside me. The driver rolled down her window an inch or two, and

TOM GAMACHE

Rocky Mountain National Park

speaking through the crack, she asked, "Is it safe to get out?" Puzzled by the question, I turned to glance behind me, thinking that perhaps a grizzly was charging my backside. Reassured that I was safe, I replied, "Sure," adding brightly, "I'm out!" "We read all about the bears," she declared, "so we slept in the car last night!" I smiled and assured them that they were safe. "It's okay," I smiled, "step out and enjoy the park!"

Thinking of that story made me recall the apprehension we feel as strangers in strange places. Those women were entering the Fearsome Land of Montana. I have just explored some unfamiliar terrain of my own, the Dreaded Canyons of Manhattan.

When venturing into strange territory, it's always good to have a guide. In my case, a longtime friend who manages the Statue of Liberty-Ellis Island Foundation came to my rescue. Before my trip to the big city, he suggested lodging and gave me tips on transportation. He provided directions and treated me to dinner. He taught me how to hail a cab. Together we traveled the subway and took a boat to Ellis Island. In the city, he was fearless, adept at conversation in the midst of noisy crowds.

In Manhattan, I always felt crowded. There are 66,940 people per square mile there! In contrast, Larimer County in Colorado is home to 97 folks per square mile. We have elbow room and lots more open space.

While I wandered through the woods, thoughts of New York drifted away. Then the distant crack of a branch drew my attention. Practically silent, yet alert, a herd of a couple hundred elk had spotted me. Bothered by an invasion of their privacy, four hundred eyes now studied my every step.

In that instant I felt like I was back in the city, with eyes everywhere. Just like those elk, I decided, people in the city tried to blend in. Almost everyone wore black, for example. This was the land of business suits and dark overcoats. Among the fashion-conscious crowds, it was clear that I was an out-of-towner, dressed in my casual khakis.

Back in the woods, I wore my usual black cap, black gloves and a black parka. To the elk, I probably looked like a predator on the hunt for dinner. For them, I was easy to spot. To me, they were a crowd of khaki.

Descending the ridge, I crossed a small valley. Until the 1930s this area had been a cattle ranch. Most traces of ranching are long gone, of course. But here, tucked beside a row of trees, I spotted an abandoned fence line. A few rusting wires and fallen wooden stringers marked the farthest reaches of a pasture. I stopped for a minute and pondered this decaying effort to keep cattle in or trespassers out.

I hopped across its remains, celebrating its destruction. The demise of a fence restored free passage for all. Today in our big cities and towns, fences are a way of life, with a mass of added security like barred windows, surveillance cameras, guards, dogs and triple-locked doors. What exactly do we fear?

I wandered on, experiencing the freedom of a fence-less land. But that broken and decaying fence stayed with me. It was dilapidated and mostly a relic, but it still troubled me. In New York I felt fenced in. In the woods I felt freedom. I wondered if those feelings were mistaken impressions or signs of our changing reality.

History shows that whatever fences our culture builds, time dooms to failure. In the long run, time has always taken civilization—and its fears and fences—with a grain of salt. Whether we wear black or khaki doesn't really matter. Nor does whether we spend our days navigating fast-paced cities or wandering peaceful forests. What does matter, however, is how we treat our fellow travelers and the land we inhabit together.

We can certainly argue that urban dwellers need the tonic of wild places. They need parks to restore their spirits, perhaps grown gray by wearing too much black. They need parks and forests as "de-fence" from the travails of modern life, allowing freedom from crowds.

We can help provide this sanctuary by ensuring that there are no signs of civilization in our wild places, no fences or citified touches. We should protect nature as it is. We should exercise our personal freedom to wander. Of course, we need places like New York City to drive our economy and enrich our culture. However, all of us—rural westerners and eastern urbanites alike—need places like national parks to discover ourselves. Sometimes it takes a visit to a city like New York, teeming with millions, to help us appreciate places offering solitude, places without fences, places like Rocky Mountain National Park.

Culture & History

"Oh, ranger, where can I see the pistol that was used to shoot President Lincoln?" It's not surprising that questions like this are asked of rangers every day. The National Park Service cares for more museum objects than any other federal agency except the Smithsonian Institution. Many things that we learned about in school are cared for by rangers: a compass used by Lewis and Clark, George Washington's Valley Forge dining tent, Ben Franklin's eye glasses, Henry Wadsworth Longfellow's manuscripts, furnishings from the homes of presidents from John Adams to John Kennedy, and even the Liberty Bell! Lesser-known but equally important objects range from 230 million year-old petrified wood and ancient cliff dwellings to John Muir's manuscripts and pioneer log cabins.

Many of the historic and culturally important items cared for by rangers are not in museums, but rather out in the parks. Forts of all kinds—frontier, Civil War, fur trader and civilian—can be visited in their original locations, places where it's possible to imagine sergeants barking out orders and the thunder of hooves as riders approached. A Minuteman II ICBM that kept many people near bomb shelters during the cold war can be seen in its original Delta 9 launch silo at Minuteman Missile National Historic Site. At parks like Tonto, Montezuma Castle and Walnut Canyon, visitors delight in the peaceful surroundings as much as they delight in viewing the remains of structures built before recorded history.

It has often been said that national parks are the best idea the United States ever had and its greatest contribution to the world. More than 120 countries have copied this uniquely American invention. Rules governing international parks and preserves vary considerably. Some contain towns and native villages; some allow hunting and even timber harvesting. All national parks the world over, however, celebrate the history and culture of their countries.

Almost as soon as Yellowstone was established as the world's first national park, work began to preserve the history and diverse cultures represented in our parks. Such efforts included the preservation and interpretation of American Indian and other native cultures.

The National Park Service and its rangers have learned a great deal since then. In the early days there were no manuals and very few policies for guidance. Rangers were little more than game wardens. Efforts to keep grazing animals and poachers out of the parks took up most of their time—whether to protect elk, giant sequoias or petrified remains of the past. After a couple of decades their jobs evolved to include visitor services. By 1928, national parks started building museums to display cultural and historic objects. More museums came along after the Depression, constructed through Civilian Conservation Corps and Works Progress Administration projects. New job titles such as "ranger-historian" and "ranger-naturalist" came into use. In the 1930s, George Wright, along with other rangers, led the way toward including resource monitoring as part of the ranger job description.

Today, parks such as Hubbell Trading Post, Pipestone and Nez Perce celebrate vibrant living cultures as the parks' primary themes. Cane River Creole, Tuskegee Institute, New Orleans Jazz, San Antonio Missions, Pu'uhonua o Honaunau, Coronado and more have been set aside to preserve the cultural diversity that makes the United States unique in all the world. Parks such as Manzanar, Minidoka Internment and the Selma to Montgomery National Historic Trail allow us to learn from the past while honoring those that they commemorate.

Rangers have always used innovative means to interpret the history and cultures of our national parks. Their resources were often limited to readily available items and their imaginations, so they combined entertainment and education from the very beginning. Nightly campfire programs were (and remain) a huge draw for park visitors. Virtually every camper would attend, sitting around a large fire, singing songs and listening to the "Ranger Talk." Rangers often played the guitar or fiddle. Even with all of our modern technological advances, today's campfire programs still hold the same back-to-basics appeal to visitors.

In 1957, Freeman Tilden authored *Interpreting Our Heritage*. It was innovative at the time and is still used today. In the foreword, National Park Service Director Conrad Wirth wrote: "Interpretation... is one of the distinctive contributions the National Park Service is making to public enjoyment and park conservation." Using Tilden's six principles of interpretation, visitor centers came into being. Visitor centers tell the natural and cultural stories using museum objects and a variety of other visual and audio methods. Dinosaur bones are no longer displayed with only a scientific explanation; graphics illustrate scenes as they might have appeared 220 million years ago. As the world entered the video and computer age, so did visitor centers, evolving to meet the needs of a more sophisticated public.

The preservation of America's diverse cultures and history is a lofty goal. National Park Service rangers play an important role, but everyone is responsible to contribute. Our national historic and cultural sites serve as an inspiration to all. They teach us about the importance of accepting other cultures and how much we can gain from understanding the beauty of our differences. Only by learning from the experiences of the past, can we help create a better future.

Oh yes, that infamous pistol used by John Wilkes Booth to assassinate President Lincoln? It's on display at Ford's Theater National Historic Site in Washington, DC.

Ghost of the Commandant's Wife

by Deb Wade

P ark rangers work with school groups and teachers all over the country. When I was at Everglades National Park in southern Florida, education rangers taught students and teachers about the habitats found in the park: dry slash pine forests; cool, shady tropical forests; sharp-toothed sawgrass glades; and the saltwater mangrove-rimmed shores and islands of Florida Bay. Soon our park's ten education rangers were asked to help the other three southern Florida parks with their school programs. We showed teachers how to camp on Elliott Key in Biscayne National Park, led city kids on night walks along wooden boardwalks over lakes full of alligators and water birds, and explored the tree islands called "hammocks" in Big Cypress National Preserve. We were constantly camping, "slough slogging" (hiking through water up to your waist or higher), snorkeling, canoeing and having a great time doing all sorts of activities with the kids.

One day, a letter came from the smallest and most remote national park in southern Florida, Fort Jefferson National Monument (since renamed Dry Tortugas National Park). They wanted help hosting schools interested in the human stories and natural history of the Dry Tortugas islands. Fort Jefferson was so remote that kids camping there would be closer to Havana, Cuba, than to the USA! Ranger Sandy Dayhoff and I agreed to make it happen. No freshwater, no food, a 132-mile drive and a four-hour boat ride were all part of the deal. Whatever we needed, we had to bring along!

Each time we headed out to Fort Jefferson, we had to be ready early in the morning in Key West. Everything we needed for three days had to be on the park work boat, the *MV Activa*, before 6 a.m. by order of Captain Cliff. If we were not ready on

VARINA PATEL

Dry Tortugas National Park

time he would leave without us—and he meant it! He knew that late departures often meant rough seas.

Most of the kids had never camped or even been on a boat. We never knew how the kids would handle the trip and the waves. Some trips, the pale green Caribbean waters would be so calm we thought we could hear the "wings" (really fins) of the flying fish that leapt in front of the bow. Other trips, we got soaked as the *Activa* bucked and tossed her way across the steep-sided waves off Rebecca Shoals.

As we neared our destination, the red brick fort and islands seemed to pop out of the open ocean. That's when our teaching began. Ponce de Leon discovered the islands in 1513. He named them the "tortugas" after the many sea turtles he took onto his ships for food. But there was no source of fresh water—the islands were dry. The U.S. military started looking at the islands in the early 1800s as a strategic location off the tip of Florida to defend our young nation from European powers. Construction of the fort began in 1846, with slaves supplying much of the labor.

We imagined what it must have been like to work and live there as a slave, laborer, soldier or prisoner. The big fort, one half-mile around, began to sink into the sand under its own weight before it was completed. Newer cannons that could pierce its thick walls were created in 1860 and used to breach the walls of a sister fort in Georgia two years later. Those cannons changed warfare worldwide and made Fort Jefferson and all brick forts vulnerable. Fort Jefferson continued as a Union outpost and prison, mainly for Army deserters. After the Civil War, in August 1865, one of its most famous inmates arrived. Dr. Samuel Mudd was sentenced to life imprisonment at the fort as one of four convicted conspirators in President Lincoln's assassination. The doctor had set the broken leg of John Wilkes Booth after Booth shot President Lincoln. Mudd survived a deadly yellow fever epidemic that killed many prisoners and soldiers, including the fort's doctor. Because of his service to the sick during the epidemic, Mudd received a presidential pardon after four years. Captain Cliff always made a point of telling the kids as we landed that some campers thought they could hear a ghost rattling chains in Dr. Mudd's old cell and that they might hear chains rattling too! But we soon forgot ghosts as we hurried to set up our tents and make dinner.

We planned to explore the coral clinging to the outer fort walls the next morning and in the afternoon the kids and teachers would write letters home as if they were

Union soldiers at the fort. But the first night after supper was for exploring the fort—in the dark.

Sandy had come up with the idea of a night walk through the old gun rooms on the second tier of the fort and an interpretive talk to bring the human connections of the place alive.

She had researched the name and history of the commandant's wife who had passed away during the yellow fever epidemic. She assembled a historic costume and 19th-century props, including a working kerosene lantern. I led the kids into the fort after dark, noting differences between their day and night impressions of the site, listening to nocturnal creatures and comparing functions of the human eye for day and night use. Sandy waited for us on the darkest side of the fort in one of the corner bastions facing the open sea. She lit the lantern to set her scene and waited to portray the dead commandant's wife, who had come back to tell us about Dr. Mudd, life at the fort and yellow fever.

That night we walked quietly, stepping cat-like along the rubble floor toward the dim orange glow in the distance. The kids were so quiet that I could hear their breathing. They figured out it was Ranger Sandy, of course, but suspended disbelief for the program and afterwards silently walked down the stone stairs to the ground level and across 100 yards of the central parade ground before they started talking. When Sandy arrived back at the tents, she had a funny look on her face, but she would not say why. It wasn't until the next trip that I understood.

A month later we took our next trip, this time with kids from West Little River in the heart of Miami. Everything went according to schedule until supper. Sandy took me aside and asked if I wanted to be the commandant's wife. I was surprised, because she had done all the work and was using her own family's heirlooms as props. But she assured me she wouldn't worry and wanted me to have the experience. I got dressed and went into the fort to set up and wait while it got fully dark. Reading our notes as it got darker and darker, it occurred to me that our story was being told directly above the old yellow fever hospital on the ground level.

I realized it was taking Sandy and the kids a long time to get there. Would the lamp run out of oil before we finished the program? I blew it out to conserve the oil. Then I heard a scratching noise. It sounded like it could be the wind blowing sand against the brick walls. Next I heard footsteps, so I hurried to relight the lantern. Nobody came.

Was it Captain Cliff or one of the fort rangers trying to scare me? I called out but no one answered. Just then a strong gust came in off the sea and the lantern went out on its own! I started thinking about all the people who had died there—slaves, soldiers, prisoners and even the commandant's wife. What if some of them didn't like rangers who came and "fooled around" where they had once lived, suffered and died? They might be angry. Very angry. So, just in case, I talked out loud about the kids, how important it was to tell the stories of the fort's people to them and their teachers. I spoke about how the inner-city students had felt a strong connection to those who constructed the fort and later, the black soldiers who manned its walls and prison. Sometime while I was speaking, the noises just faded away. I could hear the kids' voices from the fort entryway. I relit the lantern and the program went on.

After all the kids were in bed, Sandy and I went out to the dock. She asked me how I had liked giving the program. I looked straight into her eyes and saw that she had experienced the ghost too. We never spoke much about it, but every trip after that we took turns waiting up in the gunroom. I can't speak for Sandy, but after that first night, I felt very safe and accepted in the dark old fort. The lantern never blew out again and I never heard any sounds other than the wind off the sea, my own breathing and the kids as they approached—excited and eager to learn. We never said a word about it to anyone until now, not even to Captain Cliff.

Letter to Dead Soldiers

by Shelton Johnson

One day I wandered into Yosemite's research library and was talking to the librarian when I noticed an old photograph. I took a closer look at the picture and read the caption. It was a photograph of the 24th Infantry taken somewhere in Yosemite in 1899. The 24th, along with the 25th Infantry and the 9th and 10th Cavalry, were African-American Army regiments that became known as Buffalo Soldiers during the Indian War period. In 1903, four troops of the 9th Cavalry were among the first "rangers" assigned to protect Yosemite, Sequoia and General Grant (Kings Canyon) National Parks. Another four troops of the 9th followed in 1904. For me, as an African-American park ranger, seeing this photograph was like stumbling into my own family while traveling in a foreign country.

Around 1900, African-Americans occupied one of the lowest rungs on the social ladder. Most of the jobs available were menial, labor-intensive and rarely considered professional. Racial violence was common in America. One of the few paths out of this morass was through the military. The Army provided a vocation, training, room and board, and a pension. It also created a sense of self-esteem, as the uniform instilled pride in country.

I had no idea that 100 years ago the 24th Infantry and the 9th Cavalry were entrusted with the protection of Yosemite National Park. I had never read this information in any history book. But staring at me, across a gulf of 100 years, were these black soldiers who had overcome obstacles that made my challenges seem insignificant. I immediately wanted to know their names and to find out as much as I could about them. They had almost completely disappeared from Yosemite's history. If it weren't for this one photograph, would anyone even know that they ever existed?

Today, as an African-American National Park Service ranger, I want to speak to these men and tell them that they aren't forgotten. The following "Letter to Dead Soldiers" is a result of that desire.

Dear men, forgive me for not writing sooner, but I only recently discovered that the dead do not completely vanish from this earth. I realize now that death does not occur with the stopping of the heart, but when we choose to forget. One hundred years after horses and the creaking of wagon wheels, your names are air, unseen, yet moving around us. How can something as substantial as a column of 26 men riding side by side on a dusty road leave neither imprint on the ground nor sound in sky?

Someone must have seen you after you left the Presidio of San Francisco in early 1899. Is there no one in Mayfield who remembers? What about Santa Clara, Firebaugh, Madera or any other towns in the Central Valley you passed through that have people old and wise enough to remember? A century's accumulation of dust has buried the 14 days that it took for you to get to Yosemite. Even our memory of you fades under the pressure of years. Yet, there you are, astride your horses in a Yosemite that is as close as the open window of my office. Is this all that remains that can be touched: a photograph and a brief mention in a dusty old military report?

> "From records in this office I find that the park was under the control of Lieut. W.H. McMasters, Twenty-fourth Regiment of Infantry, with a detachment of 25 men of the Twenty-fourth Infantry, he being relieved June 21, 1899 by Lieut. William Forse, Third Artillery, with a similar detachment of that regiment."
>
> *E. F. Wilcox, Captain, Sixth Cavalry,*
> *Acting Superintendent of Yosemite National Park, October, 1899.*

Is this all that is left of you? All of your hopes and desires, your thoughts and dreams, your horses and wagons, even your bodies and the shadows you cast on the ground, all squeezed into the space of one sentence. To live only in a phrase, to find that all you ever were, or hoped to be, lies trapped among a procession of nouns, adjectives and prepositions. To find that the collective memory of your life has become simply a reference in a government

MARC MUENCH

Yosemite National Park

document. This is a terrible kind of eternity, but preferable to oblivion, because it means that you still live.

History has momentarily forgotten your names, but not your deeds. I know that in the months preceding your arrival, sheep and cattle were grazing illegally in the park. I know that in late summer of 1898, extensive forest fires burned in Yosemite. The smoke of those fires still seems to obscure your lives. Even the officers who relieved you could only sense your presence by the condition of the park when they arrived, and what was recorded in monthly reports to the Department of Interior.

"I am unable to find any records as to the operations of these troops outside of the monthly reports rendered to the Interior Department, but from the present condition of affairs I am convinced that the park was as well guarded and protected as possible considering the small number of men detailed for the purpose."

E. F. Wilcox, Captain, Sixth Cavalry,
"Report of the Acting Superintendent of Yosemite National Park,"
October, 1899

When you arrived in Yosemite, the stockmen noticed your presence, just as they noticed your absence in the months preceding your arrival. The demands of the Spanish-American War forced the temporary suspension of military stewardship in Yosemite. This was of little concern to sheepherders who used parklands for grazing their flocks. They knew the country better than you and ran their sheep far from the trails you patrolled. A million acres is a lot of space for 25 men to cover. In your time, it was easy to avoid the presence of other people and lose yourself in Yosemite.

These stockmen knew where you were and avoided you, but I wish the opposite. How can I reach across 100 years and hold out my hand for you to take? How can I convince people that you are not dead but live on? Not just in documents and old photographs, or even in the park ranger uniform I wear, but as real soldiers surviving into the present? Because I choose to remember you, you live on in me. I know your lives had meaning to black folks. I know that someone may have called you son, brother or father. I think I understand why you joined the army. You had few choices and a military career provided a sense of dignity, respect and, importantly, a pension upon retirement.

Understanding all of this leads me to my father. Dad grew up in rural South Carolina in the 1930s. He served in the Army and the Air Force from the 1950s until the 1970s. He is a veteran of Korea and Vietnam. Although we lived together as a family in several states—and two foreign countries—my father was absent for part of my childhood. I remember venturing into my parent's bedroom and touching his clothes. I would hold, smell and caress them as if this action would release dad from the void that had swallowed him and return him home to me.

Thinking of him leads me to a place and not just a time. I imagine the hardships he endured in Southeast Asia. I imagine the hardships you endured in America and the Philippines. Those thoughts create a pathway to you. I have made a bridge of my father and it leads to you. You too left loved ones behind who cherished your memory. You too risked your lives so that the lives of your brothers and sisters, mothers and fathers, would be better. You are more than just soldiers of the 24th Regiment of Infantry, and this story is bigger than just a chapter in Yosemite's military history. To consider it solely on that level would serve only to diminish your lives and the complexities of the country you lived in.

Thus the memory of my family's sacrifice has become inextricably bound to the sacrifices of you who are long dead, but not completely forgotten. We have met before. The face of history is never a stranger. The deeper we gaze into the past, the greater our recognition of ourselves in other places and other times. We are all amnesiacs stumbling around the world trying to find out who we are, where we come from and where we belong, until that moment we find a story that reveals everything.

You who are soldiers, who are family, have given me that story. In so doing you have ensured a presence in Yosemite for yourselves. Thank you for clearing the trail that I followed 100 years later. You cannot imagine how your passage has made my journey infinitely easier, as I hope mine will for those who follow.

Reading Stories in the Landscape

by Kate Petrie

I really enjoy working as an interpretive park ranger because it allows me to connect with people—both with the visitors I meet and the historical figures whose lives we teach about as part of the park's history. Exploring what life was like for these folks can range from reading the basic facts to exploring the woodlands, fields and foundations they called home. In a sense, we are reading the landscape they shaped with their lives.

One of the neat aspects of our national parks is that they preserve examples of the lifestyles of the typical American, as well as the famous. Along with the estates of presidents, we can find the cabin of an average colonial villager or the farm of a typical pioneer. All are preserved so we can learn how everyday people like us used to live. Sometimes we find unexpected stories as well.

Acadia National Park rangers interpret many such sites that you can visit on a ranger-guided hike or boat trip. One of the most rewarding programs, which I enjoyed leading for several years, was the exploraration of Baker Island, a small island that lies off the Maine coast. The wealth of history etched in Baker's landscape spans thousands of years! The long-term settlers of the island, the Gilley family, arrived in 1806. Their story offers us an intimate look at life in the 19th century. Hannah and William Gilley

moved to the island with their three small children. With the dream of a better life they cleared land, built a homestead, fished and farmed for survival, and laid claim to Baker Island, eventually raising 12 children!

Our group, a collection of vacationing families, began the trip to Baker Island in a large modern boat. Transferring to the island, however, required rowing ashore in a small wooden dory. Pointed

MARC MUENCH

Acadia National Park

on both ends, the dory resembled the paper hat most of us learned to fold from newspaper as children. Weighted heavily along its keel, the dory swayed from side-to-side in wide arcs, causing passengers to question its stability. Ocean water lapped at the gunnels as the captain reminded us that the boat's original purpose was to tend nets and transport the day's catch. "Everyone just sit still and act like dead fish and you'll get ashore just fine," he quipped with a grin. Just imagine what it must have been like to work all day hauling nets by hand from this rig!

Once on shore, we continued our journey, angling along a low bluff. We began to ponder the feelings Hannah and William must have had as they started out on this small patch of land. I asked my group to search the landscape for clues to the past using only their eyes; we did not want to disturb the historical story by turning over rocks or walking on sensitive plants. That would change the story and make it harder to read.

Eroded portions of the bluff exposed thick layers of pebbles and silt. It was here that someone noticed the first signs of human disturbance. Cutting across the layered pattern of soil, perpendicular grey rectangles of color could be seen. We realized they were pieces of rotted wood. Stepping back and looking at the full sweep of the bluff, someone pointed out the blotches were spaced at fairly regular intervals. The whole group tuned in as we pieced together the theory that we'd found the bases of very old fence posts that once ringed the field above. A basic discovery, yes, but a good example of how the landscape holds on to quiet clues of its past!

Rounding the bluff, we climbed up to an open field, where we intersected with a footpath that ran between the beach and the homestead. Here we encountered a benign-looking post that presented us with an odd mystery. A cement marker shaped like a square fence post about five feet high, covered in lichen, was a lonely sentinel to a field of shrubs. What was its purpose? Why was it made of cement? We continued past historical structures, learning more of the Gilley story. The island community continued to increase as the Gilley's grown children built their own farms on Baker Island.

We followed the trail up a slope through fields separated by a row of spruce trees. I asked my group to look at the evergreens and give me descriptive words for these trees. Bemused and intrigued looks crossed their faces as they played along and put their observation skills to work. We created a list, including "full growth," "symmetrical," "orderly" and "fence-like." "Okay, now look at the fields on either side of the row and describe them." We noticed rock walls, a huge pile of field stones and a small ring of stones like a garden plot. We put the landscape clues together to define the outline of two house lots.

Another cement post was found nestled within the boughs of a spruce that had grown up around it. We reached a point where we could see a tower at the top of the island, yet another clue to the past. As trade increased along the Maine coast, the U.S. Lifesaving Service determined Baker Island to be a key location for a lighthouse to warn ships of nearby ledges. In 1828 the Baker Island Lighthouse was built and William was appointed lighthouse keeper. William and his family earned a favorable reputation for reliable service in keeping the light shining through all types of foul weather and circumstances.

We visited the tower, then descended the southwest slope of the island. The path passed over thin soil and ledges. We found more cement posts. The first was broken and was projecting out of a muddy portion of the path. Short segments of iron bar protruded from a ledge along the trail. Investigating the metal pegs we noticed many more posts spreading off in two directions. The metal pegs anchored the posts to the ledge.

I must confess that, for many years, I stepped over the broken post in the trail and walked past the others without ever noticing them, until one day a child pointed them out and questioned their purpose. On a separate research trip I traced the route of the posts across the island. It took a 90-degree turn in the middle of a boggy area and boxed off the land around the lighthouse. It did not follow the landscape or any reasonable pathway. What was the purpose of this fence? Why did it follow such an odd path? History has been known to take odd turns at times.

As our nation grew, the political climate began to shift and the Whig party came into control. Even remote settlers like the Gilleys felt this shift. Lighthouse appointments were political appointments and William was not a Whig. Given his excellent service, Whig representatives invited William to join the party. The independent William declined the offer and was replaced as lighthouse keeper.

Can you imagine what it must have been like to be the new lighthouse keeper assigned to Baker Island? As you might imagine, the change in command was met with considerable angst and disharmony. The new keeper found himself in dispute with his neighbors over boundary lines and right of way to the shore. The increasing tension prompted the Lifesaving Service to challenge the Gilley's ownership of the island.

Fortunately for all parties involved, the U.S. district attorney struck a compromise allowing both the Gilleys and the government to stay on the island. A portion of the island's summit was carved out for lighthouse operations, while the bulk of the island went to the Gilleys. Additionally, access from the shore to the lighthouse would be permanently marked as "Main Street" and would be a free right-of-way for everybody. Our mysterious posts were put in place to mark the permanent Main Street and to outline the lighthouse keeper's property. Only an agency involved in a court dispute had the manpower and motivation to haul cement to an island. Eventually, ill feeling healed and the lighthouse keeper became part of the island community.

As time passed, families on the island moved to coastal areas where new amenities such as electricity were available. The dwellings on Baker Island became seasonal homes and were eventually sold. Noting the historical and ecological value of the island, a number of entities have worked to preserve Baker Island and today the bulk of it is protected as a portion of Acadia National Park.

We could read about the Gilleys' lives in books but we wouldn't get the same feeling for their story as we do from visiting the island they settled. It was finding the clues in the land itself that deepened their story. We returned from our trip tired but enriched by our experience of reading the stories in the landscape.

Land of the Free

by Barbara J. Finfrock

Gettysburg, Pennsylvania, has been the destination of American families and school groups for many years. Primarily, this is to experience the battlefield and national cemetery known as the Gettysburg National Military Park. Nearly two million visitors each year visit this park to see the battlefield and museum, and to learn more about what happened so long ago.

This park commemorates the bloodiest battle of the American Civil War, July 1 through July 3, 1863. Following those days, citizens in the small borough of Gettysburg and the surrounding farm land of Adams County lived in the horrible aftermath of war, amidst the devastation and loss of animals, crops, and sometimes parts of their houses and barns. Citizens nursed the wounded soldiers and helped to bury the dead left behind by both the Army of the Potomac and the Army of Northern Virginia.

In 1864 the Gettysburg Battlefield Memorial Association was established by concerned citizens. The goal was to preserve portions of the battlefield as a memorial to the Union troops that fought the battle. This land was transferred to the federal government in 1895, and Gettysburg National Military Park was established. After many years of administration by a special commission of Civil War veterans, care of

the park was transferred to the Department of the Interior—to the National Park Service—in 1933. The mission to preserve and interpret the Battle of Gettysburg and the story of Lincoln's Gettysburg Address to park visitors is carried out daily by park staff and volunteers.

As a volunteer in the Ambassador Corps of Gettysburg National Military Park, I had an unusual "chance of a lifetime" to see hate at work, and then the reaction to that hate. Through it all, the National Park Service and its volunteers were able to provide quality service to visitors from all over the country. The Ku Klux Klan held a rally on Saturday, September 2, 2006, in Gettysburg, legally requested and permitted in accordance with the First Amendment of the United States Constitution. There had been similar rallies held at Harpers Ferry National Historical Park—two weeks prior as the National Park Service was celebrating the 100th anniversary of the Niagara Movement—and at Antietam National Battlefield earlier in the summer.

It was chilling to see the robed, hooded Klan members waving their enormous red flag as they were escorted across Taneytown Road to enter their assigned enclosure on the lawn of the Cyclorama Building—and not just from the cold, rainy weather. I had never before experienced quite the feeling I did that day. When I looked beyond the grassy enclosure, I saw that there were snipers atop the Cyclorama Building. I think the Klan had come to realize that there is an "audience" at national parks and also an assurance that they will be protected and able to enjoy the right to assemble and speak, as permitted by the First Amendment.

I had a couple of wonderful experiences when the rally was over and the few visitors who had witnessed it were leaving. One was with a group of two young families: two dads, two moms and two kids. The parents were sorry their kids had seen the rally but were too fascinated to leave the scene. They responded very positively when I got down on the young boy's eye level and spoke directly to him, as they knew I was really talking to all of them. I said that this was a powerful learning experience that they had just witnessed. This rally was an example of what it means to live in the only truly free country in the world, where everyone is allowed to voice their opinions and is assured of a safe environment in which to do so. We may disagree with what others say but we should never disagree with their right to say it. NPS staff and volunteers had prepared a short statement about First Amendment rights to hand out, explaining what those rights really mean. Those families went away thanking me over and over for taking the time to help them understand how to deal with the day. They said they would go with their kids to school to talk with teachers about how to present such topics in the classroom. Very positive!

The next memorable incident was with a couple about 40 years old. The wife was extremely upset (in a tearful state) that such rallies were permitted, especially on such

Gettysburg National Military Park

sacred ground. I spoke with them, just trying to help her get a handle on her feelings. I told her that before I start my volunteer duties each day at the park, the first thing I do is walk the entire path through the Soldiers National Cemetery. I always feel calm and different afterwards. I urged her to do the same. We talked a bit more and then she looked at her husband and said she would really like to take that walk before they left. A little while later, she found me just inside the lobby of the visitor center and came over to hug me. She was again in tears, thanking me, saying that she would always remember how I helped her make sense of her own feelings and put a positive end to that day of hate. It gave me a good feeling inside and reminded me of why we work to preserve this hallowed ground, and about what made it hallowed in the first place back in 1863. Living in the "land of the free" came to life for me that day in a very different way.

Soldiers National Cemetery was designed by William Saunders, a prominent landscape architect and founder of the National Grange. Removal of the Union dead to the cemetery from their shallow battlefield graves began in the fall of 1863 and was not completed until 1872, long after the cemetery was dedicated on November 19, 1863. The words spoken on that day by President Abraham Lincoln are indelible in the fabric of our nation's history. Although the dedication ceremony featured orator Edward Everett and included solemn prayers and songs to honor the men who died at Gettysburg, it was Lincoln's two-minute address that has lived on in our memories. His eulogy of the Union soldiers buried at Gettysburg still resonates to remind us today, as it did to those in attendance in 1863, of the soldiers' sacrifice for the Union cause. To understand the battle of Gettysburg is to know an important part of our nation's history.

Gettysburg National Military Park has much to offer to all visitors and it is an honor to be able to serve here as a volunteer. I believe that we all share the responsibility to ensure that the cost of our freedom—and how it has been hard-won throughout history with the loss of lives and blood—is never forgotten. People should visit Gettysburg National Military Park not only to enjoy its beauty and magnificence, but also to reinforce that freedom is just as fragile today as it was in 1863.

Baskets are Life

by Julia Parker

Arriving at the age of 18, my first impression of Yosemite was not unlike those of visitors today. The first thing I noticed was the water... the sound of water and the water coming down, just flowing. I was enthralled with Cascade and Wildcat Falls. I remember turning in a big circle, looking at the high granite cliffs and water falling down, marveling at their beauty. I imagined that Yosemite might become a shelter for me, as it had been for early native peoples. Born in 1929 of Coast Miwok and Kashaya Pomo ancestry, I was orphaned at the age of six and raised in a German foster home.

The story of my interpreting Yosemite Indian culture, and my basketry, goes back to when I was a child and was sent away from my people's land. I went to Stewart Indian School near Carson City, Nevada. Every chance I had, I'd go to the museum and look at those beautiful baskets, never thinking that I would someday become friends with the willows, redbuds, fern roots and all the plants that go into making the baskets.

I have spent nearly 60 years of my lifetime working in Yosemite. I have interpreted Native American culture in Yosemite National Park from a time before rangers had the official title of "interpreter." I was apprehensive when first approached about working in the park to share my culture and craft with visitors. I wasn't college-educated, wasn't a

 descendant of the local Indian tribe and didn't know much about making baskets. However, I did have a deep knowledge of the culture; I was married to a native and was raising a family in the Old Indian Village in Yosemite. My husband's grandmother, Lucy Telles, lived with our family. I watched Lucy and learned to gather and prepare materials, make baskets and then use them in utilitarian ways for things like cooking, carrying babies and gathering acorns.

Once I learned to make baskets, I continued to make them throughout my life. To me, baskets are life.

You see, baskets are a part of life that was here and that still can be here. We may not do it exactly in the way that our ancestors did it, because you can't go back and live like our ancestors lived. But it is magnificent that those weavers knew how to balance and work those designs into the basket. My last teacher, who died about ten years ago, told me, "When you do something, do the best you can." I realized that she wasn't just talking about baskets, but she was talking about everything in life. She demonstrated baskets and interpreted our culture from the 1930s until she got sick in the late 1980s. She balanced not only the designs in her baskets but also the way she lived in the Indian and the non-Indian worlds.

It is hard to live in both worlds and make them your own. Indian ways are often different from non-Indian ways. The Indian people gather the plants and respect them. They always give offerings to the plants and say "please" to the plants and "thank you." We talk to the plants and they let us know what's going on. We each have our own gathering sites and try to respect other people's gathering sites, though sometimes people do raid other people's gathering places. I continue to gather the materials in places where my teachers—my husband's relatives—invited me to go in the Yosemite region.

A lot of our people have lost the old ways, so one of the most important things I can do is try and teach old ways. I want them to continue, because I feel that Native American women who had made these beautiful baskets have not received proper credit for the legacy of beautiful artwork they've left us. It wasn't until recently that they've gotten much recognition. It is important that this legacy be passed down not only to park visitors but also to the descendants of those women. We have to recognize that non-Indians also have helped us to preserve our culture. Collectors bought and kept the baskets, so they are here for us to see. If the collectors hadn't bought them, the baskets would probably have been burned and buried when people died. Baskets from Yosemite are in museums and private collections all over the world. When we see those baskets, we must remember that these are not just beautiful or interesting containers, but that they serve as a reminder of the people who made them.

To many native people, learning to make baskets is not just a hobby or a pastime. It is a way to connect with our ancestors, connect with the land and concentrate on good

IAN SHIVE

Yosemite National Park

things. These artifacts are all reminders of individuals. It is important to realize that we are all different people, fundamentally connected, yet each with our own stories. As an example, the women who made many of the wonderful baskets in Yosemite were wonderful women who balanced artistic careers, housework, child care and working outside the home. They were remarkable women who kept on working hard until their deaths. I spent a lot of time with these women, because I knew, liked and respected them. They were always working, making baskets, making quilts, cooking, cleaning and always doing things. The women were role models who had successfully kept their Indian ways but took the best that the modern world had to offer them. That is an important thing to remember, that native people change, like people all over the world.

I used to feel alone a lot. When all of the muhas, the grandmothers, had died, I felt alone. When I work on my baskets; though, I feel like they know I'm here. The spirits are out there with us. I used to feel very lonely when I would sit underneath the oak tree behind the museum and just make baskets. Then one of the ladies said, "You're never alone. You have the wind, you have the sun, you have the birds and you have the animals. You have all these things with you and they're your strength." I always say that I wouldn't be what I am today and couldn't weave like I do without the women who came before me. I feel like a little bit of them comes out in me whenever I make a basket.

I make baskets, demonstrate techniques, tell native stories and work as a cultural interpreter. I travel nationally, consulting, teaching and lecturing. It has been a great honor to display my work in the National Museum of Natural History, Smithsonian Institution in Washington, D.C., the Yosemite Museum, the Norwegian Ski Association Headquarters in Oslo, Norway, the private collection of Queen Elizabeth II of England and numerous other collections. In 2004, I held the first one-woman exhibition by a Native American basket weaver at the Bedford Gallery in Walnut Creek, California.

The American Indian peoples of Yosemite have more history with this land than any other cultural group. These people were real people, with families, not just storybook people when dressed up. No matter who you are or where you come from, the national park is everybody's story. My life is here and my story is Yosemite. Like all people that contribute to an ever-changing Yosemite, I feel I've touched this place and have made my mark. In turn, Yosemite has become a deep part of me. The two stories have evolved together and are deeply entwined—woven like the willow stems in one of my baskets.

Navajo Rugs

by Laurel A. Racine

The Northeast Museum Services Center is a specialized regional office of the National Park Service that serves 80 parks from Maine to Virginia. Part of my job as curator is to assist parks in finding objects for their museum collections. For several years I worked with the cultural resource specialist at Shenandoah National Park, helping to acquire furnishings for President Herbert Hoover's fishing cabin at Rapidan Camp. Hoover's cabin, called the "Brown House," is several miles downhill from Shenandoah's famous Skyline Drive, which runs 105 miles along the crest of the Blue Ridge Mountains in Virginia. Even before we started acquiring objects for the collection, we knew that the completed exhibit would be popular because visitors were already flocking to the remote location just to see the empty buildings.

Rapidan Camp was the first complex designed specifically as a retreat for a president of the United States. There are historic photographs that show exactly how the cabin looked when President Hoover used it during his term in office from 1929 to 1932. Of the hundreds of objects in the pictures, only about fifty survive today. Shenandoah officials decided that, in order for the public to understand what Rapidan Camp was like, the Brown House should be furnished to match the pictures. That meant that many hard-to-find items had to be acquired.

President Hoover and his wife, Lou Henry, decorated their retreat with many Navajo rugs, none of which remain in the park today. Since comparable rugs from the period would be prohibitively expensive, if available at all, we decided to buy new replacements for most of them and commission two of the most important ones. According to the historic photographs, two Navajo rugs had hung prominently in the main living room. One was a "Yei" rug and the other had "whirling logs," or swastikas, in the corners. Yei rugs depict figures based on Navajo deities. Including these deities in rugs was controversial at first but was accepted over time. The swastika symbol, however, is still very controversial today because of its strong association with Nazism, which began in 1933 just as Hoover's term as president was ending. Many are surprised to know that, prior to Nazi use, the swastika appeared in the art of many different cultures, symbolizing the four winds, abundance, prosperity and other benign things. We felt that the rugs were important elements in order to accurately interpret the cabin and that they should be reproduced as closely as possible.

We decided to go to Arizona to purchase the rugs that were needed and to meet with Navajo weavers face-to-face. A few years earlier, I had met Ed, the curator at Hubbell Trading Post National Historic Site, which is located in the heart of the Navajo Reservation. The site has served as an active trading post since Lorenzo Hubbell opened it in the 1870s. Ed and his co-worker Kathy knew Navajo weavers who would be able to make the rugs we needed and they arranged for a meeting. Kathy acted as a translator and was key to our success. As both a Navajo Indian and a National Park Service employee, she was able to bridge the cultural and language barriers.

The morning of our meeting we drove from Winslow, Arizona, onto the Navajo Reservation. We were apprehensive as we approached our most important task—hiring weavers to make the rugs. During the car ride, we talked excitedly about what we might expect. We were struck by the open expanses and by the few humble buildings that dotted the landscape. It was as if we had crossed into a different country. When we saw the lack of prosperity, the same thought flashed through both our minds: we would pay any reasonable price that the weavers asked. I knew that most Navajo weavers have no other source of income and, lacking formal education, have extremely limited job opportunities.

The meeting was scheduled for 10 am. We arrived early, so we went into the visitor center and introduced ourselves to the person at the front desk. Soon an elderly Navajo woman approached and introduced herself as one of our potential weavers. We held a very simple conversation in English, and she introduced us to her husband and to another weaver who was also interested in our project. Ed found us involved in conversation and

MARC MUENCH

Shenandoah National Park

moved us into his office to speak privately with the weavers.

The Navajo women had long dark hair, lightly threaded with gray. They wore simple blouses and skirts with heavy turquoise jewelry and silver concha belts. The weaver's husband held his hat in his hands and wore black jeans with a meticulous patch on the knee. I was struck by this patch, evidence of a life so different from our disposable society.

When we started talking business, we spoke to the weavers through Kathy. The women spoke for about five minutes at a time and Kathy occasionally relayed a couple of sentences to us. We responded quickly and then listened for another stretch. We understood absolutely nothing. Not a word! This was not like catching a few familiar foreign phrases on the subway and being able to guess what was being said. We really had no idea. This experience allowed me to appreciate this soft, beautiful language and to contemplate its role in World War II. During the war the military employed Navajo Marines, called code talkers, who sent battle plans as coded messages in the unwritten Navajo language. The code was never broken by the enemy.

We had thought that we would spend a lot of time with the weavers looking at the enlarged black and white photographs of the historic rugs and talking about designs and colors. That part of the meeting actually went very quickly, the women knew the designs and exactly what colors should be used. However, we spent a long time on logistics. Neither woman had a telephone, so communication with them would have to go through the trading post. There was a lot of discussion about how they would be able to afford materials for the rugs. They were concerned about not being paid until the work was complete. This was unexpected. Transactions with other craftspeople were generally focused on the item needed, with payment simply made at the end. As we tried to bridge the cultural gaps we encountered, we learned a lot about these amazing people.

After about two hours of fascinating but exhausting discussion, we hired the women to each make one rug. We then took some time to talk briefly about their lives. The weavers were curious about us, as well. They wanted to know how far we had traveled, what it was like where we lived and if we had flown over an ocean to meet them. Our questions centered on their weaving. How big were their looms? How long did it take to weave a large rug? Were they successful in selling them? The most telling thing we learned was that very few, if any, of the younger generation were weaving professionally and often left the reservation to pursue more profitable jobs.

Saying farewell and starting for home, we had lunch at the only restaurant for miles, the cafeteria at the local hospital. We talked about the experience and wondered how successful we had really been. Were we polite enough? Did we all have the same understanding of what would happen? When we checked in with Ed, he said the meeting had gone well. He was, however, surprised that we didn't negotiate, which is a custom observed in trading posts all over the world. I explained the agreement we had made before the meeting and hoped that our failure to negotiate had not been taken as an insult.

Our relationship with the weavers continued throughout the coming months. After nervously checking with the trading post from time to time, we received the two Navajo rugs about a year later. They were incredibly beautiful and fit the needs of the park perfectly. The rugs were the product of two National Park Service units and two different cultures working together toward common goals. Today, the Navajo rugs hang proudly on the Brown House walls, just as they did in President Hoover's day. These near-perfect replicas are works of art—made using traditional methods that span many generations. They are enjoyed by thousands of visitors to Shenandoah each year. I consider my experience on the Navajo Reservation, especially my enduring connection with the women who wove these magnificent rugs, to be one of the major highlights of my career with the National Park Service.

The Guardian

by Ken Mabery

Sometimes park rangers get to touch the earth in deeper ways than others. While serving at El Malpais National Monument, a park that contains a large, rugged backcountry area, I was privileged to see Mother Earth in a way that few have observed.

El Malpais literally means "the badlands," but this volcanic area holds many surprises. Lava flows, cinder cones, pressure ridges and complex lava tubes dominate the landscape. The park is intimately tied to the culture and religion of the Acoma, Navajo and Zuni tribes. Their reservations surround the park, where tribal members routinely visit shrines and other special sites. This tribal legacy adds to the story of El Malpais and challenges park rangers to protect an evolving cultural landscape. When I worked at El Malpais, much of the backcountry had not been explored or fully mapped. Researchers and rangers were continually making discoveries of varying importance—from unique plant associations to new species and geologic features, including caves.

A photographer named Harry volunteered to photograph and map many of the interesting features in the park. His primary interest was scenic and geologic features, but he also had a good eye for unusual vegetation. Late one evening I received a radio call from him. I could hear the excitement in his voice. Radio transmissions were often  poor in remote areas of the park, so I only heard bits and pieces of what he was trying to say. I could make out only enough to know that Harry had found something he deemed remarkable and was concerned that others might stumble onto it. Since the area was in a remote section of jagged volcanic terrain—and whatever he found had been previously undisturbed—I advised Harry to leave everything in its place so that we could discuss his find in person.

LAURENCE PARENT

El Malpais National Monument

About three hours later when he got in from the field, Harry came directly to my house. He was still very excited. He had found a small cave with barely enough room for two people. Inside, he saw two geometric objects that turned out to be intact prehistoric pottery bowls! He had not been able to hear me clearly on the radio, so he tried to figure out the best course of action. He knew that federal law protected prehistoric artifacts. He also knew that pothunters (illegal collectors) could easily sell these items on the black market. He reasoned that since he was able to see them clearly, others, including pothunters, might also. He decided to carefully move the bowls farther back into the cave where they would not be as visible. He reasoned that this would protect them until rangers could properly document them for the museum collection.

The cave was in an area that had been included in Acoma and Zuni land claims. The tribes had documented close cultural ties to the land, going back many centuries. Pottery vessels could be identified as Acoma or Zuni based on easily recognized characteristics. The park's policy was to consult with tribal officials before moving or removing anything of cultural significance. Out of respect for American Indian traditions, this consultation process was conducted with the fewest possible people involved.

Harry had to return to work that evening, so he sketched out a map and provided detailed directions to the site. Early the next morning, I packed an electronic monitoring device and headed out with Darwin, another park ranger. Meanwhile, the superintendent set about contacting Acoma and Zuni's tribal officials. Despite Harry's detailed instructions, it took us over four hours to locate the cave. While rigging a warning device that would transmit a signal through the park's radio system if anyone came into the area, we noticed what appeared to be fresh disturbance to a nearby "cairn." A cairn is a pile of rocks, stacked on top of each other, that is used to mark a trail or other feature. For example, early miners built cairns to mark the corners of their claims.

When we got home that evening, I called Harry to let him know that we had a protection device at the site and mentioned the disturbed rocks. He said that he had knocked over a rock cairn so that it would not attract others to the site. My heart sank. Every volunteer had been instructed not to do any damage to anything. In this area, rock cairns often dated back to prehistoric times. They are almost always culturally significant.

For the next month we sat on pins and needles while elders from the Acoma and Zuni pueblos decided which tribe claimed this site. After it was determined that it was part of the Acoma heritage, a time had to be scheduled for five elders to visit the site. On the day of the visit, the elders, a translator, Ranger Darwin and I approached the site. The silence in this remote area was broken only by the sounds of our footsteps and breathing. When we were still a mile from the site, the elders started talking in whispers that increased in volume while they were pointing at the ground. For some, the excitement included mistiness in their eyes. I couldn't imagine what could be causing this excitement. Finally, the translator dropped back to where Darwin and I were respectfully walking.

He told us that the elders had noticed a special plant growing along the trail. "They have not seen this plant for generations over on the reservation. They thought it didn't exist any more. It has very important medicinal properties for men, especially older men," he said.

Since the plant was common in the park, we started talking about the possibility of collecting seeds to propagate plants for traditional uses. Excitement remained high for the last mile, despite a steep climb across the slopes of the volcano. I began to feel that the park was on the verge of a significant opportunity to make a contribution to the tribal culture. I had often talked with elders about traditions that were dying out. Here we had the chance to help bring back an important element in the practices of their medicine men. One elder who had always been very reserved approached me and very solemnly shook my hand. My heart swelled with excitement. A way of life that was more than a thousand years old would be enriched by our trip into the wilderness.

When we were in sight of the cave, silence fell over the group. The elders stopped dead in their tracks. Ever so quietly, the senior elder directed a short question to the translator. After a short silence he turned to us, "What happened to the rock cairn?"

I had neglected to mention it to any of the party. My voice was shaky as I explained Harry's actions. As the translator relayed this information, I could see a progression of confusion, dejection and heartbreak on the faces of the group. Discussion started amongst them. From their tone, I sensed that this was a private tribal matter and respectfully moved away. No one had even looked into the cave.

Hours later the translator sought us out. We had explored the area surrounding the site and were quite some distance away. The elders were still conversing in a tight group near where the cairn had been. The translator pulled us aside and started to explain. His voice was hushed and full of emotion.

According to well-known traditions, to help the mountain breathe, their ancestors had placed the pots in the cave. They had also built the "Guardian"—the rock cairn—to ensure continued protection of the offering. The Guardian was the most important part of this tradition and this site. A chill crawled up my spine as I heard this. The elders knew the blessings and offerings necessary to reposition the pottery vessels—that part was straightforward. The prayers and traditions to repair the Guardian; however, were completely lost to them. Tears welled up in the translator's eyes as he went into detail. Without the Guardian, he explained, the offering in the cave could not help the mountain.

For another hour or so, discussions continued about what might be done about the Guardian. I have never felt so close to the spirit of the earth, and yet so removed. The mountain beneath my feet was solid rock, yet I was feeling unsteady and disconnected. Although the pottery vessels could not do their job without the Guardian, the elders decided to leave them in place until other prayers and preparations could be completed back home. There was hope that these activities might reveal something about rebuilding the Guardian. As we walked back through the area of plants that had caused such great excitement just hours before, all were silently absorbed in reflection.

Afterwards, I found it difficult to patrol that section of the park without reliving the emotions of that day, when I had the privilege of being exposed to the deep-rooted American Indian ties to Mother Earth. I had the opportunity to open new doors of trust with tribal leaders and gained a greater understanding of their cultural beliefs. It took many months for the Acoma elders to determine a course of action to put things right on the mountain. Although we never knew what ceremonies and prayers were required, we know that it was a long and involved process. I can only hope that the Guardian has now been properly restored.

From that experience, rangers at El Malpais gained a deeper appreciation of the significance of the many cultural sites we protect. The preservation guidelines of the National Park Service took on new, more deeply personal meaning. To this day, the experience touches my heart and influences my every effort to protect America's cultural, natural and historic resources.

Search & Rescue

Lost in a Wonderland of Rocks
- JOSHUA TREE NATIONAL PARK -

Misadventure at Grand Canyon
- GRAND CANYON NATIONAL PARK -

The Little Pickerel
- ISLE ROYALE NATIONAL PARK -

The White House is Calling
- ROCKY MOUNTAIN NATIONAL PARK -

Two Brothers Overboard
- CURECANTI NATIONAL RECREATIONAL AREA -

Six Feet Under
- LASSEN VOLCANIC NATIONAL PARK -

Stories about National Park Service search and rescue missions date back to the late 1800s—there was a Yellowstone visitor who fell into the crater of a geyser, a climbing party in distress on Longs Peak at Rocky Mountain National Park and three women who spent a cold night on Columbia Rock at Yosemite before searchers brought them to safety.

There have been innumerable dramatic calamities since then: an adventurer who parachuted onto Devils Tower with no planned way down, the perilous rescue of a climber from the 2,700-foot vertical face of Grand Teton, a helicopter that crashed upside down into the Colorado River at the Grand Canyon and a kayaker who plummeted over a waterfall at New River Gorge National River.

The earliest park rangers were expected to be bold and courageous, endangering themselves to bring visitors to safety. In the words of Horace Albright, the first superintendent of Yellowstone, our first national park, "Risking his life to save that of another is something that every ranger must be ready to do, any time he is called upon." He went on, "Visitors to the national parks unfamiliar with trails and with mountain climbing often overestimate their endurance or their ability to find their way through the forests." Rangers have always warned visitors against taking unnecessary risks and some visitors continue to take them anyway.

In the 1950s, the Army's elite 10th Mountain Division influenced NPS search and rescue operations. Their quick response with specially trained and equipped men was legendary, but their gear was heavy and unsophisticated. Technical rescues of people on cliffs used a piece of rope tied into a loop to make a sling. Old photos show rescue baskets and litters made with two poles and a piece of canvas.

By the late 70s, recreational users were flocking to the parks and rescue equipment had been improved. Litters were made of lightweight fiberglass, safer and more comfortable. Stronger nylon ropes were developed. Major climbing parks, such as Mount Rainier and Yosemite, changed to these ropes by the late-1970s, with other parks following in the mid-1980s.

Today's search and rescue rangers carry only essential, lightweight gear for greater mobility. Everything from flashlights to first-aid kits has continued to evolve. The most advanced equipment includes special night helicopters equipped with forward-looking infrared to detect body heat.

Search procedures have changed, too. In the 50s, rangers used a typical military search technique: line up lots of people and search every inch. What worked for military rescues wasn't appropriate in parks. Lost soldiers acted differently than civilians with no survival training.

In the 1970s and 1980s, behavior was studied and searchers tried to understand the lost person, not just cover the landscape. They began to keep records of how far away victims were found from where they were last seen. Searchers weren't deployed outside that perimeter unless solid clues were found. Searchers held interviews with people who knew the lost person. By the 1980s many professionals agreed that a successful search wasn't only about strength and numbers; it required brains, too. The emphasis was on training, good techniques and emergency medical training.

Today's park rangers perform thousands of search and rescue missions each year. Millions of visitors flock to national parks and inevitably some become lost, stranded or injured. There are hiking mishaps, cave rescues, wilderness searches, mountaineering accidents, crevasse rescues, avalanche operations, surf rescues in the Atlantic, Pacific, Gulf and Caribbean, and treacherous missions on high, snowy peaks in Alaska.

Visitors, of course, are given precautions and safety tips. Rescue is never a certainty! Warnings include information about good judgment, adequate preparation and constant attention. Backcountry users should be in good physical condition, prepared to survive on their own. Appropriate equipment and knowledge of how to use it are essential for a safe trip. Public education programs focus on teaching people to stay safe while enjoying the wilderness. In particular, programs focus on teaching young children what to do if they get lost in the woods.

Hikers are told that their safety is their own responsibility—know your route and the weather forecast, tell a friend about your plans and always take basic safety items, even on short hikes. Recommended gear includes plenty of water and food, a flashlight (plus spare batteries and bulbs), whistle, lightweight rain gear, compass, signal mirror, watch, extra layers of clothing and first aid kit. Importantly, hikers are told never to rely on cell phones, as reception in the wilderness is not reliable and, even if you can place a call, you can't rely on a rescue, which could be difficult or impossible due to weather conditions or terrain. In the wilderness, you must be self-sufficient!

Every day, rangers put their lives on the line to save the lives of park visitors in trouble. Whether you're a casual day hiker or a mountain climbing enthusiast, a few simple precautions will help you stay off the list of victims. Learn from the lessons and mistakes of others, and you'll have wonderful adventures in our national parks.

Lost in a Wonderland of Rocks

by Judy Bartzatt

Spring had arrived in the desert and the day was warm and sunny. Marvin and his son, Mark, had been enjoying the park all day, stopping to take pictures and explore the overlooks and trails. By early evening they had made their way to the Barker Dam area in the interior of the park. Barker Dam is situated in an area called the Wonderland of Rocks, a twelve-square-mile maze of enormous boulders with steep drop-offs and deep crevasses that pose significant danger to an unaware hiker. Marvin and Mark parked at the trailhead, where a sign told them Barker Dam was 1.5 miles ahead. They decided to walk to the dam but, just for fun, they would take different trails. Misreading the sign, they wrongly believed that the two trails looped back together at the dam. Marvin took the trail to the right—which was actually a connecting trail passing an archeological site and then on to another trailhead—and Mark took the trail to the left, which went directly to Barker Dam. As they separated, neither of them thought about taking a jacket, water or a flashlight, which are all critical when hiking in a desert environment. It was still daylight, the temperature was warm and they believed it would be a short, easy walk before they were reunited at the dam. They were unaware that the two trails did not loop back together and that lack of proper preparation would turn a short hike into a life-changing experience.

After taking the trail to the left, Mark walked the mile and half and arrived at Barker Dam. The problem was that he didn't see his father there. Thinking that maybe he'd just walked more quickly, he waited about an hour before getting nervous and deciding to head back and report his father missing.

On the other trail, Marvin hiked about a mile before he

MARC MUENCH

Joshua Tree National Park

realized that it was not looping back toward Barker Dam. He saw a large boulder and rock field, but he could not find the trail. He decided to climb up onto the boulders to get a better vantage point from which to look for his son.

Back at park headquarters the following morning, my workday was just beginning when I got a call from one of the law enforcement rangers. They had spent the previous night looking for a man who was missing in the Barker Dam area. As the chief ranger, I immediately drove to the site where a command post had been established and the incident command system organized. The incident commander told me that Marvin had not been seen since he and his son separated the night before. Rangers had been conducting the initial stages of a "hasty search," in which rescuers walk the area of last contact, calling out the lost person's name. I was also told that Marvin's wife, Mitz (pronounced "Mit-zee"), was on her way from their home. I enlisted the help of the park's Public Information Office, which coordinates with the media to present accurate information to the public. This is key, as one of the standard search procedures is to close off the search area so rescuers won't be mislead by other visitors' footprints or unrelated signs that could inadvertently lead rescuers in the wrong direction.

That same morning, the San Bernardino County and Riverside County Sheriff's Offices began working with us, which provided a large group of volunteers to assist. We had people on the ground, on horseback and in helicopters—using heat detection sensors—searching the area where Marvin had last been seen. As night began to fall, the temperature dropped and the wind began to blow. There had been no sign of Marvin, who would be spending his second night alone, left to survive in the wilderness. This was difficult to report to Mitz, but we also knew it was still early in the search and that there was a good possibility we would find him. We left crews at the parking lot and left vehicle lights on to help provide direction in case Marvin was trying to find his way back. The search parties returned to the incident command center in the evening, as searching anything but the main trails after nightfall is dangerous and rarely productive.

The search continued over the next three days without any sign of Marvin. Mitz was at the command post every day. She encouraged and thanked the searchers continually. She even started to empty trash containers and clean the tables where the searchers ate their meals. I tried to get her to rest, but she always said, "I want to do something to help the searchers." She was a profound inspiration.

As we pulled the searchers out of the field on the fourth night, it was becoming increasingly difficult to maintain our hope of finding Marvin. The weather had been very cold each night, but the temperatures were rising during the day. It was critical that Marvin be found, if indeed he was still alive. We had not seen any signs of movement by him whatsoever—torn clothes, for instance, or shoe prints—and almost 100 searchers had been looking in the thousands of crevices in the Wonderland of Rocks.

The incident command staff decided to bring in over 200 searchers over the weekend. We all knew that we needed to find Marvin soon if he was to have any chance of survival. Realistically, by the weekend, the statistics suggested it would turn into a recovery mission. That Thursday night I went home and prayed that we would find him. I hoped not to have to tell Marvin's family that we were going to have to scale back the search and reorganize as a recovery effort. This is the last thing that any ranger ever wants to do.

Friday morning the searchers arrived for a briefing and got their assignments. One search team, the Riverside Mountain Rescue, had just gotten their first assignment on the incident. They were given coordinates for a search location. The team entered the coordinates into their GPS unit and a helicopter dropped them at the search site. After the helicopter left, the team members noticed that they were not precisely at the assigned location. They reentered the coordinates and set off in the right direction, which required some pretty tough climbing because of the difficult terrain. While moving slowly through the Wonderland of Rocks, one of the team members called out, "Marvin!" This is a technique used by searchers who are hoping that the lost person will hear them. When she shouted again, she heard a moan come from a nearby crevice. She looked down into a 30-foot hole between two big rocks and saw Marvin lying on the ground. He had a broken ankle, had suffered a concussion and was severely dehydrated, but he was alive!

Back at the command post we heard the team call on the radio. They had found Marvin and needed a helicopter to transport him to safety. I wanted to make sure we were hearing them right. It was hard to keep my emotions in check while waiting for confirmation that Marvin was indeed alive. It was an immense relief to be able to tell his family that the rescue team was preparing Marvin to be flown to the local hospital.

Marvin had fallen 30 feet into the crevice the first night. He was below two large rocks so he could not signal to the helicopters or the searchers. He was in critical condition and was told later by doctors that he probably would not have survived one more night if he hadn't been found. Yet he had survived, defying all the odds, trapped alone in the wilderness for five days and four nights! Fortunately, Marvin had drawn on survival skills learned in the military. He had covered himself up with sand each night in order to stay warm and avoid the severe hypothermia that could easily be brought on by the cold desert nights. This was critical in sustaining himself and also in warding off the worst effects of dehydration.

Marvin still does not remember much about his experience that week in the desert and prefers to deflect attention to the rescuers. Mitz stays in regular touch with me and the many others involved in Marvin's rescue. He's the "miracle" of my career. I treasure the enduring friendship that I now enjoy with Mitz.

In my role as a law enforcement ranger, I am involved in many situations that affect people's lives, both positive and negative. It's wonderful to be able to recount a situation that involves such a happy ending. Marvin's rescue and his family's unwavering hope is something that I'll carry with me for the rest of my life, a source of strength to draw on anytime I must embark on a new search and rescue mission.

Misadventure at Grand Canyon

by Nancy Eileen Muleady-Mecham

In early July, Todd traveled to the Grand Canyon from Indiana to join his friend, Brandon from New Mexico. They drove along the East Rim and stopped at Grandview Overlook. There, the trail to Horseshoe Mesa was an open invitation and the two friends decided to go for a short walk down the Grandview Trail. It was steep but deceptively easy. Each carried a 12-ounce bottle of sports drink. After three miles, they were out of fluids. Todd decided he would continue down to the Colorado River. He estimated that it couldn't be too far away and would catch a ride with a boat crew to Phantom Ranch to the west. While he couldn't see the river from the trail, he was convinced that going further down into the canyon towards the river was their best bet. (Perhaps he just wasn't ready for the long, inevitable hike back up to the rim.) Brandon wasn't keen about the idea. He thought going back up the three miles of trail was safer. Todd went off-trail to climb a ridge to figure out the quickest way to continue down to the river. The choice became easier when the two became separated. Brandon lost site of Todd, and after a long wait, began the steep hike back to the trailhead alone, hoping his friend would soon follow.

Brandon made it back to Grandview Overlook and waited for Todd's return, ultimately spending the night in the car. The next day, at 3:30 p.m., with canyon shade temperatures at 114 degrees, Brandon finally alerted the rangers that his good friend was missing. A search immediately commenced, spearheaded by a reconnaissance flight over the area where Todd was last seen. At 1,300 feet above the flat Tonto Platform, the helicopter spotters thought they saw something in Cottonwood Drainage. In a narrow crack, a figure was spotted lying still on a rock. It was about a mile from the river, in an area of steep cliffs and dry falls. It was 50 feet from the top of the crevice to the rock below, with no immediate place for the helicopter to land. When it finally landed several miles away, Ranger Chuck hiked in to the crevice where 26-year-old Todd lay badly injured. Ranger Matt and Volunteer-In-Park (VIP) Tim soon followed with additional gear. Darkness was falling when the helicopter returned with additional rescue personnel, placing Rangers Nick and Tammy on the western access point and me to the east. Nick and Tammy worked their way down to the patient. The rescuers in the crevice could not communicate directly with the rangers on the rim because of the high walls, so I remained on the Tonto Platform as the radio relay. The helicopter was not allowed to fly after dark because there are no lights in the canyon and had to return to get ready for the next day's transport needs. I was left alone on the plateau with my paramedic bag, personal survival equipment—including two quarts of water that I always carry in my bag—radio and an extra gallon 'cubitainer' of water to get me through the night.

Another radio relay, Mike, was at Grandview Point, near the trailhead. He would relay all of my information to the incident commander at park operations on the South Rim. Chuck called up a patient assessment to me to relay to Mike and then on to the base station physician at Flagstaff Medical Center. It was apparent to Chuck that Todd had fallen almost 50 feet onto a slab of rock. He was mentally altered, his skin was hot and dry to the touch, and he was ashen-colored. His eyes were glassy and his mouth was dry. He complained of being dizzy and spoke in only two to three word sentences. He had blood on his scalp and blood dripping from his nose and mouth. Chuck heard diminished lung sounds on one side. His temperature was 104 degrees. He had pain in his neck, chest, abdomen, and feet, and had begun to cough up blood. He'd had only 12 ounces of fluid in 24 hours. Chuck started an intravenous (IV) fluid drip and used his own drinking water to wet Todd to cool him out of his heat stroke. He gave him oxygen intermittently from his one cylinder.

Chuck and I talked sparingly to preserve radio batteries. In between these conversations, I stood up on the Tonto Platform and looked around. There was no one else for miles. I was truly alone on the nearly flat ground. A short distance from the edge of the crevice was a single rock about two-feet high and two-feet long. This rock was the only upward solid projection among the soft bushes and short grasses. I watched the sun set amidst

MARC MUENCH

Grand Canyon National Park

gathering monsoon clouds, which made for a brilliantly-colored display. Lightning flashed somewhere in the distance and I could hear the distant booming of the thunder.

The rescuers prepared Todd for evacuation, taking precautions to immobilize him in order to protect his neck and spine. In the morning, the rescuers would need sawyers (people who work with saws) to cut vegetation, along with extra personnel to help carry Todd to safety. They had scouted the river drainage before dark and there was a 60-foot cliff that would require moving Todd a short distance by helicopter. Known as a "shorthaul," Todd would be lifted into the air at the end of a rope under the helicopter and then taken to a second, specially equipped, medical helicopter waiting on the river. A motorized boat would be required to carry Todd across the river to the nearest safe landing zone (LZ) for the medical evacuation helicopter.

Once I had relayed all of the information, we agreed to check in with each other every fifteen minutes, conserving battery power in between by turning off our radios. With my radio off, I was cut off from civilization and the scale of the huge plateau really set in. I could hear nothing but the wind and the wisp of the bushes with their small branches rubbing against each other. I heard the scurry of a mouse. As I reveled in the immense wilderness, I picked up on a disturbing pattern in the sky above. The distant lightning was not so distant anymore. Strikes began to hit within two to three miles of my position. I saw the strike, started my count, one thousand one, one thousand two, etc., with every five counts before hearing the thunder equaling a mile. It was still a bit off, but coming my way. When I checked in with the crew below after midnight, I found myself talking to Tammy.

Apparently there was a situation developing that could have serious consequences. The rescuers had used most of their drinking water to cool Todd, who had stabilized. Now the rescuers were starting on that quick road to dehydration. Tammy said they would start IVs on each other to stay hydrated. She asked how I was doing. Relative to them, I was in pretty good shape. I was on the wide-open plateau with a cooling breeze approaching. My only concern was lightning. The tallest thing within a mile of my position was that small rock, so I was a bit concerned about being struck. We wished each other good luck and signed off until the next check-in. The clouds closed in over my last glimpse of the Big Dipper.

Using plastic garbage bags that I kept in my paramedic rescue bag, I made a poncho.

I did this just as the sky opened up and the rain began to fall. Lightning and thunder clapped all around. I crouched down, lying on my left side with my back against that one little rock and my paramedic bag against the front of my torso. It was the best I could do. I was still the highest thing around. A few times I saw the lightning, and before I could even start counting, the thunder split my eardrums. It was spectacular. I remember thinking that, in other circumstances, I would really be enjoying this spectacular display of nature. I tried to make myself as small as possible. Tammy knew that I might not check in if the lightning got bad, because handling a radio in a thunderstorm would have turned me into a lightning rod. I was worried about her and the other rescuers being at risk of dehydration and she was worried about me getting hit by lightning. Finally the brunt of the storm passed and I was able to check in with Tammy. We both expressed relief at each other's survival.

In the morning, it got warm really early. As I talked to the other rescuers, they sounded exhausted. All were suffering from dehydration. At 7:30 a.m., Mike relayed that the helicopter was on its way. I passed that information to the rescuers in the crevice and then strained to hear the distinctive whir of the helicopter.

Ranger Dave was brought in by helicopter to the north side of the Colorado River, where he assembled his boat and ferried additional rescuers across the river. Todd was much easier for the sawyers and litter-bearers to reach by going up the Cottonwood Drainage. That way they didn't have to hike across the Tonto and then rappel down into the crevice. By 1:00 p.m., Todd was placed in a rescue litter, which looks like a long basket, and then the litter-carry crew began to maneuver him down the canyon's drainage. The litter-carry team consisted of six people at a time, who carried Todd by brute force over uneven terrain for a long distance. The work was taxing, so the teams changed out often. At the cliff face, Todd was prepared for the shorthaul. He was lifted into the air at the end of a rope under the helicopter to an LZ downriver where the medical evacuation helicopter waited to take him to the hospital. He was treated for a broken bone in his neck, a collapsed lung, two broken feet, a broken right elbow and internal injuries. Amazingly, Todd lived and, in the end, all of the rescuers were safely evacuated.

While this story has a relatively happy ending for Todd (after all, he survived!), his unfortunate circumstance certainly took a large toll on both him and the park. Over 55 National Park Service personnel contributed to help rescue Todd, at a cost of nearly $60,000. The necessary rescue efforts also created damage to the park's natural resources, which, like Todd, will take years to fully recover. Yet, his situation could have been easily prevented by taking a few simple precautions, which any ranger would have gladly explained had he and Brandon simply checked first at a visitor center or ranger station before embarking on their adventure. No doubt, it's a lesson Todd, Brandon and, hopefully, all those who hear their story, will never forget!

The Little Pickerel

by Michael P. Ausema

Isle Royale National Park, on Lake Superior, is no stranger to fierce storms, but occasionally, a really memorable one comes along. One summer afternoon, a particularly ferocious storm rolled in quickly. Suddenly the sky was full of pounding thunder and wind-driven rain. With a racing heart, I sprinted down the steps of my cabin to my floundering boat. The Pickerel, a little 14-foot, 30-horsepower boat, was being pulled into the angry sea. The wind nearly flattened me and rain pelted my face as I ventured out from the protection of the trees and into the full wrath of the gale. The winch system, which normally pulled the boat up onto the shore, had already been dragged into the frigid water and the Pickerel rammed continuously against the rocks of the shoreline, making sickening smacking sounds. I leaped into the water and dragged the heavy winch system up on land, then inch by agonizing inch pulled the water-logged boat from the lake. For the next hour, I bailed bucket after bucket of water until the boat sat upright again.

When I finally had a chance to look around, I could just catch a glimpse of the open water of Lake Superior beyond Middle Islands Passage. The scene sent a shiver down my spine. Waves as tall as houses rolled in and crashed onto the rocky islands, sending spray high into the air. Even in the protection of the harbor, I could see whitecaps in every direction. The temperature hovered in the mid 40s. It was hard to imagine that this was the second day of July!

It was already late afternoon when I ventured a quarter of a mile down the trail to Daisy Farm, the largest backcountry campground on Isle Royale. The three-sided wooden shelters were filled with shivering, drenched campers. At least half of them were wearing only cotton t-shirts, better suited for a stroll in the tropics than the beaches of Isle Royale. A few hearty souls attended my evening program about loons, which I presented under the cover of a shelter that evening. Afterwards, several of the campers returned with me to my cabin for some dry blankets and hot chocolate.

It was 10:30 p.m. and the forest and lake were completely dark. The last few campers had left my cabin, heading back to their own shelters. I was exhausted and surprised to hear a knock on my door.

"Are you the ranger here?" asked a quivering voice. Two bedraggled campers nearly collapsed on the floor. Before I could say anything, they continued, "We just hiked three and a half miles from Moskey Basin because our friend there is hypothermic and having trouble breathing. Please, can you help her?"

I began calling on my radio in an attempt to get backup from either Rock Harbor or Mott Island. The calls were met with silence.

"Well, if you don't mind helping me push my boat back into the water, we can go to Moskey Basin now," I replied hesitantly.

Outside, rain continued to fall heavily and whitecaps churned in the harbor. With the help of the two campers, we inched the Pickerel back into the water and were soon on our way to Moskey Basin. The next time I tried the radio, I connected with Rock Harbor, and a ranger promised to be underway within minutes. He had a much faster boat and ended up passing me on the way. His lights helped me find the dock and with four extra hands on board, I was able to tie the boat to the dock in the heavy chop.

On the far side of the campground, we found the hypothermic woman. She was gasping for air and was extremely pale. She was beyond the point of shivering. We decided to bring her out of the campground on a rescue litter, which looks like a long basket, and get her to the electric heat of Rock Harbor as soon as possible. We carefully wrapped her in warm, dry blankets and began the difficult job of carrying her on the litter along the rough trail to the waiting boat. It took six of us an hour to carry her the half a mile to the dock. The two campers thanked me and then plodded back to their tents. By the time I got the Pickerel's motor started and had turned around to return to my cabin, I could barely see the distant light from the rapidly retreating rescue boat.

Soon I was utterly alone in the midst of a raging Lake Superior storm. Darkness enveloped me as I bounced over the whitecaps into the wind and driving rain. All sense

MARC MUENCH

Isle Royale National Park

of direction abandoned me. The journey back to my cabin would have to be navigated with equal measures of instinct and luck.

It was then that the seriousness of my predicament hit me. Moskey Basin is quite wide, but a mile or so down the channel I would encounter an area referred to as the Narrows. During the day or with radar, it is easy enough to pass through, as long as boaters stay in the center of the channel. However, I had neither radar nor daylight to guide me. On either side of the Narrows there are sandbars and submerged rocks that could easily end the life of a boat. Waves were splashing against the bow and I had to continuously wipe the rain from my face. I slowed the Pickerel to a crawl and turned my running lights off to improve my night vision. Each minute that passed felt like an eternity. Suddenly, trees loomed right in front of me. A sick feeling overwhelmed me as I realized that I had veered too far to the south. I was nearly on top of the submerged rocks!

I turned the boat hard to the left and listened for the telltale crunch that would indicate the tragic end of the Pickerel (and me!). Miraculously, I didn't hear it. The boat continued to putter toward the north, bringing me back to the middle of the channel. Cautiously, I continued to inch along toward Daisy Farm.

Just when I was beginning to lose all confidence in my directional skills, I saw a faint light on the northern shore just a couple of hundred yards away. I was almost home! Unfortunately, since I had pulled my winch system onto the shore, there was no safe way to tie up the boat at my cabin. The main campground dock was just a quarter of a mile away, so I headed in that direction instead.

Again, I slipped into the gloom. Creeping forward, I knew the dock was right in front of me, but I just couldn't see it. I swung my flashlight back and forth trying to catch a reflector. Finally, a metal cleat glinted in the darkness. With a huge sense of relief, I grabbed the dock and in the blink of an eye had two lines firmly attached. It was nearly 2 a.m. by the time I finally turned down the little path to my cabin.

The next day the storm lifted and sunlight filtered through my cabin windows. I learned that waves had been measured as high as 15-feet tall on the open lake and that the wind force was listed as a "strong gale," which equates to between 47 and 54 mph. The hypothermic camper made a complete recovery and life for all of us returned to normal. For me, it was all just another day at the office.

The White House is Calling

by Doug Ridley

Joe, the chief ranger, looked at the telephone receiver in his hand with a quizzical expression. Was the White House really on the line or was his staff up to another one of their practical jokes?

Rocky Mountain National Park's mountainous panorama, glacial moraines and alpine tundra beckon over three million visitors annually. The more vigorous outdoor enthusiasts leave their automobiles behind. These intrepid visitors come to hike the trails, seek solace among the peaks and valleys and push themselves to dizzying heights, far from civilization and deep in the backcountry.

It was just such an experience that Cheley Camp employee Hayley sought. At age 16, Hayley had come from her home in Tennessee to work at the eastside youth camp in the summer of 1995. She enjoyed hiking the trails, bagging 'Fourteeners' (climbing peaks over 14,000 feet in elevation) and showing the boys at camp that she could keep up. One of the unwritten rites of passage—primarily among testosterone-charged young men—challenged employees worth their salt to complete what is known as The Mummy Kill. Rangers call it the Dance in the Dark or the Ypsilon Death March. A successful Mummy Kill requires a solo hiker to traverse the Mummy Range, including the six

summits of Chapin, Chiquita, Ypsilon, Fairchild, Hagues and Mummy mountains—all in one day! The average height of these peaks is 13,255 feet and this 16-mile, cross-country trip is not to be taken lightly. Physical strength and stamina are required. Map and compass skills and the ability to travel long hours in steep terrain in the dark are absolute necessities. By August, Hayley felt that she was ready. She was physically fit, had all the necessary survival gear and understood the challenges of the route... or so she thought.

The ranger's day at Rocky Mountain seldom ends the way it begins. Daily activities are typical of large western parks: law enforcement, EMS, resource protection, fire, and search and rescue missions. During an average year there are about 200 incidents that require ranger assistance. Even on busy days when visitors are idling at entrance stations, campgrounds are full and radio traffic is frantic, rangers keep an ear tuned for the rescue call, anticipating a plea from the unknowing, ill-prepared or just plain unlucky. So it was on August 10th at 6:30 a.m. when the dispatch office received an overdue party notification that triggered a two-day search for Hayley.

As the district ranger for the Fall River and North Fork areas, I was downing my third cup of coffee, trying to decide whether to wear my dress or field uniform. Class A dress is typically reserved for those quiet days when I attend meetings, work on budgets or improve my report writing skills. I opted for the Class B field uniform with the hope of serving the public by getting out of the office and maybe even getting dirty. When the phone rang at the Bighorn Ranger Station, the call was to inform me of an overdue report. Hayley had departed Chapin Pass trailhead the morning before, at 3:30 am, alone and in the dark, intent on completing The Mummy Kill. Her visiting parents had camped out in the Roaring River drainage, anticipating her appearance there last evening. She never arrived. They waited beside the trail in sleeping bags until first light and then hiked out to contact a ranger.

Determining search urgency is based on many factors, including terrain hazards, subject profile, experience, available equipment and weather. As I arrived at the operations center I assumed the role of incident commander, a search team of one. Based on available the information, I determined the search for Hayley to be urgent. The terrain was horrible, she carried limited equipment for multiple nights out, her knowledge of the area was questionable and she was alone! The weather factor was the remaining catalyst for an urgent response. Weather had been typical for August, with late afternoon thunder and lightning, gusty winds, and snow and hail above 12,000 feet.

I gathered an incident command team to manage the search. We activated several field teams, some with dogs, to try to trace Hayley's steps from the point last seen. We searched her intended path from the end of the trail at Horseshoe Park and focused on areas where previous cross-country hikers had become disoriented. Field teams

MARC MUENCH

Rocky Mountain National Park

concentrated on the Roaring River trail, Chapin Pass to the summit of Mt. Ypsilon, and the egress points toward Mt. Fairchild, the most difficult part of the traverse. All this would take time. A U.S. Forest Service helicopter would conduct three sorties, flying the intended travel route and inserting teams for positioning. The search team now numbered 45.

Most of the Search and Rescue incidents are resolved within the first 24 hours. This time we were not so lucky. Despite the best efforts of rangers in the field, search dogs, helicopter pilots, observers and command personnel, Hayley was nowhere to be found. The command staff segmented the search area and brainstormed all possibilities for Hayley's location. Fortified with take-out pizza and hot coffee, we settled in for a night of planning and speculation. The next morning came quickly. By now, the search team had grown to 75. The helicopter was temporarily grounded due to weather. Field teams were deployed with instructions to stay out all night if necessary.

Searches for lost people have the potential to become epic events. While outside pressures have no effect on the missing subject, they can indirectly influence search urgency. Concern from relatives and demands from the media sometimes create an unwelcome burden, adding to the already high level of stress that accompanies any search and rescue mission. The longer an incident lasts, the more public interest is generated. As a consequence of this publicity, unusual offers for assistance or advice often come in, such as palm readers, clairvoyants, and anyone with a sixth sense or premonition. Over the years, I thought I had seen it all. I had this in mind when Joe came by the command post and asked to speak with me privately.

Joe looked like he'd just passed a kidney stone. "Doug, I just talked to the White House about your search. They want to make sure this one has a favorable outcome."

"Yeah right chief, that's a good one."

"I'm not making this up," he countered without a hint of a smile.

You see, humor is often used in the ranger ranks to relieve tension, especially in a situation like this. Rangers love a good scam and Joe can hold a straight face with the best of them. He struggled to convince me that the phone had rung minutes before in his office and a no-nonsense voice said, "This is the White House, please hold for the Vice President." Three things went through Joe's mind: 1. What's Ridley up to now? 2. Who's on the phone pulling my leg? and 3. Dang, what if it really is the White House?

As it turned out, the Gores were close personal friends of Hayley's family in Tennessee. The Vice President was calling to offer any necessary assistance and, shall we say, lots of unbridled encouragement.

I wished that it had been me that had called Joe's office claiming to be the White House! Once I realized that Joe wasn't kidding, I thought, "I don't care who is calling, we're going to go out and do what we've always done. We've got a group of talented professionals and they'll push the edge of the envelope until we find this girl!" One remaining concern was whether or not to relate the White House connection to the incident team. The field teams had enough to worry about without adding to their stress. Fortunately it wasn't long before we received some welcome news.

To the relief of family, friends and (I'm sure) Vice President Gore, Hayley was located deep in Hague's Creek drainage that afternoon. Searchers, directed by the helicopter, heard a shrieking whistle and followed it to Hayley's location at treeline. Her story unfolded at the debriefing. A hailstorm had forced her to abandon Ypsilon Ridge and to seek shelter in the trees. She selected what seemed to be the safest descent, but one that drew her northwest toward Desolation Peaks, away from our primary search area. To her credit, she did what lost people are supposed to do—she hunkered down in one spot, used pieces of clothing to signal the helicopter and a whistle to attract the attention of searchers, and carried enough gear to survive two cold, wet nights alone in the Rocky Mountain wilderness.

Afterwards, we boasted to ourselves that the political interest generated by this successful rescue would pay big dividends for years to come. Not me! I'll be happy if we never hear from the White House again... Ever!

This story is dedicated to Ranger Jeff Christensen and the men and women who conduct emergency operations on all our public lands.

Two Brothers Overboard

by Bob Cornelius

It was Memorial Day weekend in 1979 when Curecanti National Recreation Area in Colorado practically blew off the map. The forceful winds kept me busy rescuing boaters. Several had been blown sideways and then capsized in big standing waves below the power plant at Morrow Point Dam. I watched as one raft was caught up in a tornado-like whirl that sent it bounding down river like a superball bouncing on a linoleum floor. Electric motor, battery, tackle boxes, lunch sacks and life jackets dropped into the drink with every flip of the raft, as the owner stood helpless with mouth agape at the rocky launch point.

I was both glad and relieved when late afternoon approached and the boaters left for the day. Before unwinding with the 20-mile commute over Cerro Summit to my home in Montrose, I met with one of the seasonal rangers. He had spent the afternoon on Morrow Point Lake, above the dam. He told me that the wind had been high and steady and that the dozen or so boating parties on the lake had mostly stayed in camp for the day. A few had found protected coves to try their luck with the big trout or kokanee.

Morrow Point Lake is a very isolated, fjord-like reservoir, located within Curecanti National Recreation Area. There is no boat ramp. Boaters have to hand-carry their boats

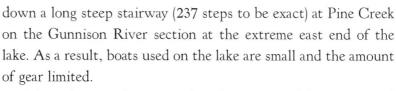

down a long steep stairway (237 steps to be exact) at Pine Creek on the Gunnison River section at the extreme east end of the lake. As a result, boats used on the lake are small and the amount of gear limited.

My wife greeted me warmly when I arrived home. We had dinner and settled in for a quiet evening. Just before midnight, I was startled from my sleep by the telephone. I staggered down

LAURENCE PARENT

Curecanti National Recreation Area

the stairs, still in a fog, and recognized the chief ranger's voice on the other end. He had been called by Ron, one of the few hardy locals who routinely dragged a boat up and down the Pine Creek stairs. Ron had loaned his small ten-foot aluminum fishing boat to two friends from Gunnison, who happened to be brothers. Although the brothers were outdoor types, they did not have experience on Morrow Point Lake.

Ron knew about the great fishing and the wilderness camping opportunities of the lake. He also knew of the potential dangers in such an isolated area. He had made arrangements to pick up the brothers at the Pine Creek Trailhead in the early evening. When they didn't arrive on time and it started to get late, he became concerned. He was in a near panic by the time he called the chief ranger at 11 p.m. that night.

Hearing the news, I too shared Ron's concern, especially in light of the high winds that I had experienced during what was now the previous day. I was also aware that the temperature outside had dropped to below freezing. I shared my anxiety with the chief and was emphatic that we should go looking for the two brothers immediately. If they were in trouble, morning might be too late.

I gathered warm clothes, a thermos of hot coffee and my park radio, then hit the road to Cimarron. I had tried to awaken a seasonal ranger, Tim, by phone before I headed out, but discovered that he was a very sound sleeper. When I arrived at Tim's quarters, I pounded my fist purple on his front door until he finally peered bleary-eyed through the screen. He had a perplexed look on his face and mumbled something about it being one o'clock in the morning. I told him that we were going on a boat ride and that I'd explain the details as we drove to the top of the dam. Hurriedly, he began to get dressed while I grabbed some big WWII sleeping bags, a first-aid kit and a couple of large canvases from the rescue cache located at the nearby maintenance shop. I raced back to get Tim and we set off for our moonless boat ride.

As we discussed the situation on our way to the boat dock at the top of Morrow Point Dam, Tim remembered the two brothers. He recalled checking their fishing licenses and campsite in Kokanee Bay during his patrol of the lake 12 hours earlier.

We dragged our extra equipment toward the boat dock. To access the dock we had to climb down a 12-foot metal ladder that was bolted to the penstock. The rungs were frosty and balancing our gear was quite a juggling act. I planted my right foot on the wooden dock and, through the cloud of my frozen breath, noticed the mop used to swab out our boat was frozen solidly to the planks. Seeing the mop and thinking of the two brothers who might be in peril added to the urgency of our task.

I stepped behind the operator console and prayed that the two 115 Mercury engines that powered our 22-foot Boston Whaler would start. To my relief, the big outboards roared to life and a cloud of exhaust dissipated slowly over the water in the cold, still, early morning air. I was glad to know that the treacherous winds of the previous day were now just a memory.

Tim untied the lines from the cleats and we motored off into the inky, cold, Colorado night. Our boat was not equipped with a searchlight, but we were able to use the docking lights mounted in the bow to feel our way along. Tim operated a hand-held spotlight from the front of the boat. It enabled us to see from side to side. We began our way along the rugged north shoreline where most of the camps were located. We dodged the ever-present driftwood for over an hour, until we reached the last place Tim had seen the two brothers. We were in Kokanne Bay and the camp area was deserted. We assumed they had headed for the take out at Pine Creek, five miles to the east, as they'd planned with Ron. We continued motoring up the lake.

We entered the Narrows on the east end of Kokanee Bay. The Narrows gives a river-like appearance to Morrow Point Lake, although it's actually a reservoir. High, sheer cliffs swallow up any shoreline. The cliffs march up canyon as two walls that uniformly dive directly into the lake. I prayed once again, this time that the two had not run into trouble in this unforgiving portion of the lake as a result of the high winds on Memorial Day.

We continued east, and as we approached a slight bend in the shoreline walls, Tim and I both exclaimed simultaneously, "Did you see that?" The beam of a flashlight had broken the black of night. It was 3:30 a.m. We made a beeline for the spot. There, perched on a precarious, seemingly pencil-thin ledge of rock, the two brothers stood uncomfortably shoulder-to-shoulder. I edged the boat up to the tiny ledge and, with assistance from Tim, the two were able to climb into the bow of our whaler. We bundled the two men into the heavy sleeping bags, covered them with canvas tarps and turned the boat back toward Morrow Point Dam. One of the brothers, Larry, was very talkative, but the other was eerily quiet all the way back to the dam. Hypothermic, he uttered only one sentence during the entire ride: "I'll never go boating for the rest of my life."

Larry explained that the two had headed out for their meeting with Ron. The wind was high but steady, and they made slow but constant progress up lake with the little five horsepower motor. As they rounded the bend, where the Curecanti Needle first comes into view, they were hit with a tremendous combination of whirling gusts and wind shear. The bow of their little boat pitched into the air, flipping end over end. They were thrown into the ice-cold water of Morrow Point Lake. They both grabbed their life jackets as they unglamorously exited the boat, and Larry ended up with a waterproof flashlight in his jacket pocket. Miraculously they spotted and were able to swim to the only possible place to crawl from the frigid water. With great difficulty they climbed onto the tiny, tilted ledge. The two stripped off some of their clothes, which they dried by holding out like flags in the brutal wind. That was at five o'clock in the afternoon, over ten hours before we found them.

The two brothers didn't want an ambulance to meet them at the dam. They chose instead to be reunited with Ron, who returned them to Gunnison. Before leaving, Larry told me, "You saved our lives. We were so exhausted that if you hadn't arrived when you did, one or both of us would have fallen back into the lake and drowned!" Hearing his words really drove home the point of just how precarious their position had been. Sometimes I wonder if Larry's brother kept his vow to never go boating again. I'll always carry the memory of that long, cold night with me, as being able to help save lives is just one of the many rewards I think about every time I reflect on what it means to me to be a ranger.

Six Feet Under

by Michael LaLone

I have seen many winters at Lassen Volcanic National Park. The winter of 2000 was an exceptionally heavy snow year. Snow had been falling almost every day and by the last week of January, the unusually deep snow pack was unstable. Those daily snowfalls never seemed to have a chance to settle and consolidate, and I knew that this made for extremely dangerous avalanche conditions on many of the park's popular ski trails. Park staff and volunteer ski patrollers had monitored the condition of the snow and—throughout most of January—we had set the avalanche danger as high to extreme in an attempt to discourage backcountry travelers. Over the years, I have come to know that some visitors will heed our advice, while others will forgo our safety warnings in order to enjoy a rare sunny day in Lassen's pristine wilderness.

Dennis and David were part of a group that had enjoyed winter camping for many years. Their careers as pastors left them little time to indulge their love of the wilderness and their enjoyment of winter camping. They greatly looked forward to their annual "ski madness weekends," which typically included five to ten friends. They picked a different area for the trip each year. In 2000, only the two of them were able to go, but they eagerly anticipated the time outdoors together anyway. They planned to ski five miles the first day, climb 10,500-foot Lassen Peak the next and return home on the third day. Weather forecasts called for snow on that last day.

At first, all went as planned. But after a successful ascent of Lassen Peak, the storm settled in much earlier and heavier than expected. Their equipment was adequate, and they considered spending an extra night and waiting for the storm to blow over, but after some discussion, they decided to ski out as they'd originally planned.

Early Sunday morning, the two men packed up and prepared to ski out to their car. After a hurried Sabbath prayer, they set out. It had snowed at least three feet during the night, and they knew they had to traverse several avalanche-prone areas. When they reached the first, both tied avalanche cords to their belts. These are generally thin, long, brightly-colored cords that are tied to backcountry travelers and allowed to string out behind. If buried in an avalanche, hopefully enough cord will be left above the snow to allow a victim to be found. These have largely been replaced by electronic transponders, which send out a signal that can be rapidly traced. Neither of the men had transponders.

Dennis and David separated from each other by the recommended minimum distance— 40 yards—and skied through the falling and wind-blown snow. Then suddenly Dennis turned back and shouted what sounded like, "Time to advance." David's vision was obscured by the snowfall, but he assumed that Dennis wanted to trade places and skied ahead. He peered through the blinding white storm looking for Dennis, but found only his tracks, which ended in a huge pile of jumbled snow. He realized that Dennis' last word had been "Avalanche!" and not "Time to advance." With a sinking heart, he immediately understood that his friend had been buried beneath the snow!

He realized that his next actions could mean life or death for Dennis. He used his cell phone to call his son in the nearby town of Chester, telling him to call 911 for help. He then began to frantically dig for his buried friend. Their only shovel was on Dennis' pack, so David used his hands in a fruitless, four-hour struggle.

Kurt (another park ranger) and I were both on duty that day, which happened to be Super Bowl Sunday. We had stopped at the chalet, an old unused downhill ski lodge at the southern park trailhead. Earlier, we had spoken with volunteer Nordic ski patrollers Frank and John, who planned to ski in the immediate area of the chalet for the morning. The weather conditions were harsh. There were strong winds and the snow was falling at the rate of one inch every hour.

At around 12:30 p.m., we received a call from emergency dispatch that a man had been buried in an avalanche. We decided to immediately activate the incident command system. Kurt was to serve as incident commander and I was to be the on-scene operations leader. Additional help was immediately requested, which included more rangers from

TOM GAMACHE

Lassen Volcanic National Park

other areas in the park, maintenance personnel and Tehama County Search and Rescue staff. We had also asked the volunteer Nordic ski patrollers to assist, although our initial attempts to contact Frank and John were unsuccessful.

We all knew that time is one of the most critical factors in the survival of a person buried in an avalanche. Once trapped, the probability of survival drops sharply after the first 30 minutes. In this case, the victim was believed to be buried several miles beyond the trailhead, with deep, freshly fallen snow between the trailhead and the avalanche scene. Foot travel would be slow and strenuous, but we had no way of knowing when the over-snow vehicles would arrive. Taking these thoughts into consideration, we decided that I would lead a hasty team (a quickly gathered group with training, experience and gear) to the scene immediately, with more help to follow when available.

After equipping myself with a pre-packed avalanche kit (shovel, probe, stove, etc.), I began to snowshoe toward the avalanche scene. After two hours of snowshoeing through thigh-high snow, Frank and John caught up with me and began tramping down the snow ahead of me, or "breaking trail," which made it easier for me to move along. Our team of three continued to Windy Point, which was two miles above the trailhead on the approach to the accident scene. The two over-snow vehicles then arrived and I briefed the team of Stuart, Curtiss, Mark and Claudia. Claudia's search dog, Nikaya, was with them.

I climbed aboard the over-snow machine to re-warm and replace the batteries in my radio while Frank and John continued on to the avalanche scene. On arrival, they met with David. He was mildly hypothermic and still trying to find Dennis by digging with his hands. They warmed him, reassured him and moved him to the over-snow machine as soon as we arrived.

We immediately determined where Dennis was likely to be buried, assembled probes to use in the search and formed a line. Avalanche probes are six to ten-foot long, thin aluminum poles, designed to be pushed through the snow as deeply as possible until they strike an obstruction. After several minutes of probing, Frank's probe struck a buried object. A second probe also struck something. Nikaya was brought to the site. She immediately caught a scent and began digging, which gave us hope. Everyone quickly and carefully joined in. We soon found Dennis' gloved hand, several feet beneath the surface.

As quickly as possible, we worked to free Dennis' head from the snow and then, unbelievably, we heard the muffled sound of hard breathing. Dennis had beaten the odds and was still alive after being buried for over six hours! We had to dig for an additional 45 minutes before he could be completely freed. He had been found six feet below the surface, hypothermic and semi-conscious, but alive. He was taken to the over-snow machine and moved to the chalet, where an ambulance waited to transport him to the hospital in Chester. I learned later that his core temperature was a life-threatening 89 degrees when he arrived at the hospital. Yet by 10 p.m. that evening he was awake and able to carry on a conversation.

After nine hours of intense effort, the team was also transported to the trailhead. We were all grateful that this search had turned out to be a rescue and not a recovery. We learned through follow-up interviews exactly how this incident had come about.

Dennis and David survived when the odds were against them. This rescue emphasizes several key points for winter survival. In addition to being well prepared for snow camping, each wilderness traveler (and rescuer) should be equipped with avalanche survival equipment, including a transponder, shovel and probe. Weather forecasts should be checked frequently and used conservatively in making decisions. Before actually leaving a trailhead, local conditions should be determined, including areas to avoid and general snow conditions. Although David's cell phone was instrumental in getting the help they needed, cell phones are not reliable for reception in mountainous or remote areas. A transponder would have helped rescuers pinpoint the right spot to dig. In my conversations with David and Dennis, I learned that Dennis had acted in the best possible way to enhance his chances of survival. He "swam" in the avalanche to stay as high in the debris as possible. When the avalanche began to slow, he moved his head about to create an air pocket before the snow pack settled. One of the main things that helped Dennis to survive was his ability to remain calm. As he drifted in and out of consciousness, this enabled him to conserve what little air he had. I am proud to have been part of the well-trained and prepared team of professionals and volunteers that had the determination and skill to reach these two very fortunate survivors.

Fire!

Red-Carded & Ready
- HOMESTEAD NATIONAL MONUMENT OF AMERICA -

Freezing Cold Fire
- SEQUOIA NATIONAL PARK -

Fire in the Swamp
- EVERGLADES NATIONAL PARK -

The Trapper Fire
- GLACIER NATIONAL PARK -

The Lookout Tower
- LAVA BEDS NATIONAL MONUMENT -

For generations, it was believed that forest fire was the enemy of our beautiful parks and forests. In 1937, President Franklin D. Roosevelt began a campaign to protect the forests from fire. During World War II, with resources at a premium, posters distributed throughout the country cried, "Forest Fires Aid the Enemy" and "Careless Matches Aid the Axis." Fires were fought with every resource available. Rangers and other brave firefighters emerged as American heroes, fighting to save the beauty of the forest and the habitat of wild animals. They climbed tall mountains, slogged through snake and alligator-filled swamps (yes, fires can burn in wet areas), and worked untold hours to stop fires. They endured heat, smoke and canned food that was packaged for the military (called C-rations), often sleeping on the ground for a few brief hours before beginning another day of battle.

In 1950, a bear cub was burned in a wildfire in the Lincoln National Forest in New Mexico and became the national symbol of the destructive force of fire. Named "Smokey," the little bear healed and grew and lived out his life in the national zoo in Washington, D.C. His caricature, dressed in a ranger hat and blue jeans, shovel in hand, glared out from posters, billboards, brochures, lapel pins, pencils and more. His widely publicized warning, "Only YOU Can Prevent Forest Fires," was known by children and adults nationwide. Smokey even had a song, which generations of young park lovers enthusiastically sang. Media coverage of forest fires showed blackened, dead trees; exhausted, sooty fire fighters; and dramatic footage of towering flames. Firefighting tools, from Pulaskis (a tool that resembles a combination of an ax and a hoe) to helitankers and other specialized aircraft, provided added excitement and drama. The media used words like "destroyed," "consumed," "blackened" and "devastated" to describe a burned area.

In the 1950s and 60s, a few dissenting voices began to be heard. Rangers, researchers, and others talked about the odd growth patterns and unusual effects of disease that they saw in protected forests. Tree species that had been doing well were deteriorating. Seedlings and young trees were few or nonexistent. Crowded forests were becoming more homogenous, meaning that there were fewer different kinds and sizes of trees to be found. In some areas, such as sequoia groves, no trees younger than 50 years old existed. Foresters voiced concern about the amount of fuel (leaves, needles, branches, logs and more) that was building up on the forest floors of national parks and forests nationwide. In forests where every fire had been fought for generations, fuels had accumulated to dangerous levels. Rangers worried that if a fire began in a protected area, it would be impossible to control. Was firefighting actually hurting the forest? Studies showed that insect infestations and diseases, which are always present at some level, can thrive when a forest is under stress, and that without fire, stress was rising. Too many trees, too much undergrowth, too much "duff" (decomposing pine needles, leaves and other debris), too little sunlight and too much competition for water and food all combined to put forests at risk—all caused by our best intentions.

Some trees cannot reproduce without fire. Some cones, such as lodgepole pine, will not release their seeds unless they are exposed to extreme heat. Their cones are coated with a resin that must be melted or cracked before the seeds inside the cone can be freed. Others, such as the sequoia, have seeds that must fall on mineral soil in order to take root; falling on inches-deep duff ensures an early death for the seed. Fires can clear a forest in a way that allows the wind to disperse seeds, spreading new trees over a wide area. Satellite images of forests after fires show that many acres inside the border may only be lightly or moderately burned, or even unburned.

A few people started to consider the possibility that lightning-caused fires should be allowed to burn in designated areas, and that fires should be deliberately set in other areas under exacting conditions—conditions that they hoped (and planned) would mimic natural fire. Believers in so-called "prescribed burning" explained that fire was a natural, necessary part of a healthy forest. The "prescription" includes weather information (temperature, wind, humidity), fuel loads, timber types, slope and more.

In 1988, a fire at Yellowstone National Park provided a wake-up call to the entire nation. In one of America's most beloved, protected and visited places, nature showed who was really in control and made it clear what could happen after so many years of fire protection in the forest. Even though Yellowstone staff had begun allowing natural fires to burn in 1972, fuels had built up, and when conditions were ripe, fires in the Yellowstone area started, grew and defied the efforts of firefighters for many weeks. Media coverage was extensive, and fire was, once again, widely described as destroying the forest, consuming trees, devastating the landscape. As with many other huge fire "complexes"—inside park boundaries there were multiple fires in the same timeframe—the Yellowstone blaze was too big, too hot and moved too unpredictably to be contained.

One of the worst of these fires, called the North Fork fire, was started by a man with a permit to cut firewood on U.S. Forest Service land southwest of Yellowstone. A single discarded cigarette butt ignited a blaze that eventually burned all the way to Mammoth, about 60 miles away! Investigators who studied the fire's behavior were able to follow its trail upwind to the ignition spot, where they found the cigarette butt. Armed with the list of woodcutters with permits and forensic evidence from the saliva on the cigarette, they were able to apprehend the culprit. Unfortunately, the damage was already done.

The work to understand the role of fire continued in earnest nationwide and a public education campaign gained momentum. The park service not only educated people about what we'd learned about fire, but also counteracted decades of legend and misinformation. Most people, especially the owners of homes and businesses near the forests, were not eager to embrace what became known as the "let it burn" philosophy. But the Yellowstone fire, with all its media attention, taught the public a lot about forest management and the need for fire. Television viewers could see with their own eyes what had happened to one of America's most beloved places after generations of fire suppression. And they learned that some fires simply can't be controlled or extinguished by people. Only the coming of cooler weather and damp conditions can put out an inferno like the one that eventually included 248 fires and burned 1.2 million acres in the greater Yellowstone ecosystem.

Historically, natural fires (started by lightning) probably occurred in most forests every ten to twenty years. Tree rings in downed trees show evidence of burns in the past and the dates can be closely estimated. Many trees have evolved to withstand fire. Sequoias, for instance, have very thick bark and the lower limbs tend to die off after years of being shaded by the limbs above. Only the higher limbs remain, usually well above the reach of the flames. Some other trees have deep roots that are not damaged by a surface fire and new trees can sprout from those roots. Hundreds of seedlings can be found in sequoia groves where prescribed burns have taken place. The bark of the huge trees may be black and scarred, which causes some concern from park visitors, but most of the trees remain healthy and strong, unharmed by this unlikely friend, fire.

Firefighters know that most wild animals can survive during a fire in their habitat. Some move out ahead of the fire, then circle around, returning to areas that have already burned. There they are safe again. As always, in nature, the strongest, fittest and smartest survive. The very young, weak or sick animals often are the ones who die. This is part of what's called "natural selection," which means that whole species stay strong when only the fittest survive and procreate. Nature's ways may seem cruel sometimes, yet the animals that die in a burned area serve as food for other animals. Nature does seem to know best. After a fire, new green tender shoots provide lots of food for a wide variety of animals. Deer, bear, rabbits and others dine to their heart's content on all the new grass and shrubbery. Plants that need lots of sunlight suddenly abound, as the shade caused by too many small trees is eliminated.

After many years of public education, fire is now beginning to be generally understood as a healthy and normal part of a dynamic forest, but we still don't have all the information we need. It took us a long time to realize that all fires are not bad. Now we need to find out if prescribed, careful burning is always a good thing. For instance, we don't yet know enough about what prescribed fire does to soils, invertebrates (bugs and spiders), amphibians (frogs, lizards, snakes) or the food web (who eats what). We don't know much yet about just how hot we should allow prescribed burns to get. We know that without enough heat, some benefits are lost, and with too much heat, damage can be done. Each forest has unique aspects and requirements that can change from season to season, and much remains to be learned. We must also accept that managing fires, even carefully prescribed ones, is not an absolute. We can never assume that we can control such an unpredictable force of nature.

Park management philosophy has changed. Once we fought nature or tried to change or tame natural processes. Now we are trying to learn from nature and to allow ecosystems to function without human interference. Is this the best way? In a time when natural areas are so impacted by outside influences (such as poor air quality, acid rain, climate change), is it possible, with a hands-off approach, to restore and preserve parks and forests? The answer is: we don't know. Studies are underway that we hope will provide some of the answers, and the search for the best possible way to preserve these breathtaking places continues.

Red-Carded & Ready

by Susan J. Cook

When people and homes are in jeopardy from wildfires, everyone does whatever they can to help make a difference. I chose to go west and fight fires on a federal interagency fire crew. A mother of two small boys, I am ten years older than most crew members. I have been red-carded for a decade, which means that I have passed all the training, physical fitness requirements and medical evaluation necessary to become a member of a 20-person crew working on a fireline.

I am a park ranger at Homestead National Monument of America in Beatrice, Nebraska. My main duties are to work with visitors and school groups. I also serve as a firefighter and assist with the maintenance of the tallgrass prairie. The prairie needs fire to stay healthy and vibrant, so a portion is intentionally set on fire each year—known as a prescribed burn—in order to help maintain natural cycles. Managing prescribed burns in prairie grass is totally different than fighting forest fires. Boy, was I about to get a quick lesson!

The fire season in the year 2000 was severe. Resources were spread thin and firefighters were desperately needed all over the country. Once my name was released to the Interagency Fire Center, I was likely to be dispatched immediately. On assignments

for large fires, firefighters like me often end up helping to protect land managed by multiple government agencies—such as the USDA Forest Service, U.S. Fish & Wildlife Service, Bureau of Land Management and the National Park Service—as well as state lands and private property. As a result, we often work with many other federal personnel, as well as state and local fire departments, and even crews from prison systems.

WELDON SCHLONEGER

Homestead National Monument of America

Anticipating very little advance warning, I packed and awaited instructions. Two members of the Beatrice Fire Department had recently completed training and were to join me. As expected, we got the call and had ten minutes to get on the road. It would take a ten-hour drive to meet our assigned crew in the Black Hills of Wyoming. A park vehicle was not available and there was no time to rent one, so we all piled into my brand new family van—which was only two weeks old—and hit the road.

After we met the crew, we followed their bus through a maze of winding dirt roads heading up into the mountains. I was amazed that my van could handle the rugged terrain. We could see the red glow of flames in the distance and wondered about our assignment. We arrived at the campsite at 10 p.m. and were told that our wake up call would be at 5 a.m. I didn't have a tent or sleeping bag because Homestead's supply was exhausted and we expected a fire cache (supply area) to provide them when we arrived. Wrong! I spent two very cold nights curled up on the back seat of my van using sweatshirts as blankets. My fellow firefighters from Beatrice had tents and sleeping bags, so they were in great shape. On the third night, I finally got a sleeping bag and slept under the stars. It doesn't sound all that bad, but the slope of the mountain can make you slide if you're not careful. That night, I woke up with a fellow firefighter's boots in my face. I soon learned little tricks to keep from sliding, like putting my arm around a small tree as an anchor while I slept.

Five o'clock was an early wake up call. After a bumpy 45-minute ride up the mountain in a military personnel carrier that fit all 20 of us in the back, we spent 14 hours digging fire line. I thought I was in good shape, but I am still not sure how I made it through those first few days. After a while, I got accustomed to the grind. To dig an effective fire line, the crew must clear a seemingly endless path about two feet wide, digging down to the bare dirt using hand tools similar to axes. With each person doing a little, a lot gets done. If you don't get down to bare dirt, the fire can spread through roots. While working on the incline, we heard a loud noise and I looked up to see a large tree rolling toward me. I was directly in its path and knew instantly that it would kill me if I didn't get out of the way. I will never forget the sound of it rolling and crushing everything in its path. I jumped to the side and pushed my squad boss out of the way. The tree hit my pant leg as it rolled on by. My crew boss and I looked at each other in wide-eyed astonishment. It was unbelievable that neither of us got hurt.

That episode was still the talk of the crew three weeks later on our way home. Everyone reveled in recounting how "I almost bought it the first day out." Five people were taken off the mountain that day with leg injuries or heart attacks. Every muscle in my body hurt, including the small muscles in my fingers. After only one day, I wondered what I was doing there and how would I survive the 21-day assignment.

The next few days mimicked that first. It didn't seem to get any easier. Each day began at 5 a.m. with breakfast, the 45-minute ride in the personnel carrier and then an hour hike up the mountain carrying everything needed for the whole day, including water to fight the fire. There was no water available past the end of the dirt road, so it was carried up on our backs. While working on the mountain, our squad boss noticed a little tuft of green in an otherwise brown area. He retreated to the personnel carrier and came back with a long pipe, which he banged into the ground next to the green tuft. Water dripped out. He then returned again to the transport and brought back a giant black tarp.

We worked for hours to build an artificial pond as a water source. We carried large rocks and built a three-foot high wall with a 14-foot diameter around the pipe! We lined the circle with the plastic tarp. The next morning we returned to find the pond full of water, surrounded by tracks from many different animals. It was great to know that we helped the animals and, even more importantly, that we no longer had to carry water on our backs for that long hike each morning. Although we were making good progress building the fire line, we still needed additional assistance, as the fire was headed toward nearby homes.

We needed help from above! My crew boss called in helicopter support. It was exciting to hear the communications between the pilot and my crew boss. The helicopters dipped their buckets in a lake and then maneuvered over the fire, dropping 500 gallons of water at a time on targets that we flagged. Our crew boss gave coordinates. All personnel were moved a safe distance away, as the powerful drops posed a real danger. One landed on a healthy, towering tree and knocked it to the ground in an instant. We were close enough to feel the cooling mist from the water. It felt great, since the temperatures reached around 100 degrees during the day.

Part of our assignment was to protect a rocky cliff interspersed with vegetation. Given the difficulty in accessing this wide swath of the mountain, we needed another way of stopping the fire from spreading. My crew boss called in additional air support, this time from a retrofitted B-52 bomber, to drop slurry. Slurry is a red, soapy substance that retards fire. What a sight to see the white bomber flying against an expansive blue sky, dropping a layer of red over the rocky mountainside! During one drop, the pilot was off by a few degrees, which meant that our crew had to scurry to escape from being slimed. We didn't quite make it and my hard hat still bears a bright red reminder of that day.

I had many amazing experiences working on that fire. I learned a lot about myself and what my body can withstand when tested to the limit. I stood on the top of two different mountains watching helicopters work below me. It was amazingly peaceful, even though a dangerous fire was moving our way. I felt such pride and accomplishment, especially as we drove down the mountain. The road was lined with property owners and community members who were waving "thank you" signs and cheering us on. That feeling, along with the personal satisfaction that comes with a job well done, gave meaning to the time away from my own family.

My homecoming was also quite memorable. I arrived a day earlier than planned, just in time to surprise my father on his 70th birthday. My parents had been worried sick about me during the three-week assignment. My sons thought I was the coolest mom ever and my husband was also extremely proud. I had such great anticipation, walking up to my parents' front door. I rang the bell and my father answered. As soon as he saw me, he began to cry. My mother was crying too. I was back with my family, safe from danger. It was so good to be home.

Freezing Cold Fire

by Carrie Vernon

When people think of forest fires—what we in the National Park Service call wildland fires—they imagine high temperatures, big flames and chaotic conditions. Believe me, I've certainly worked through my share of scorching hot days on uncontrolled fires. Ironically, two of my favorite fire memories took place in the freezing cold.

One November day in 2006, I shivered my way through a prescribed burning operation in Sequoia National Park. I was at 7,000 feet elevation and in a helicopter with no doors. Why, you ask? Well, because I was actually igniting the fire.

The prescribed burn was planned for an area near Cabin Meadow and the purpose was to reduce dead vegetation on the ground. This kind of fire is designed to protect park resources in the long term. Lightning fires can be catastrophic when too much fuel has been allowed to accumulate. Because of the steepness of the terrain and the size of the area, the burn boss in charge of the operation decided to light the middle of the burn from the air. Using helicopters is often safer and more efficient than using firefighters on the ground, who would have to climb rugged, dangerous mountains to light the fires by hand.

Lighting from the helicopter is done using a device called a Plastic Sphere Dispenser (PSD). The PSD uses spheres that look like ping pong balls. The spheres are filled  with potassium permanganate and are sent down chutes where they are injected with antifreeze. The two elements combine, which causes the balls to ignite. It takes about 20 seconds for the reaction to occur, so the balls should reach the ground by the time they catch on fire. This can be a high-risk operation, but through good planning and training, we use the PSD safely. It also happens to be really fun. Our helitack crew often argues over whose turn it is to work the PSD.

For the Cabin Meadow burn, it was my turn. Before we took off on that chilly, overcast morning, we removed the helicopter doors, got instructions from the burn boss and loaded up. I sat in the back seat, with the PSD machine jammed between me and the pilot. In addition to my safety harness and protective gear, I put on every layer of clothing I could find. I felt more like a kid wobbling around in a snow suit than a firefighter.

The seven-minute flight to the burn area was cold, made worse by the outside air whipping through the cabin. As we approached the burn, I looked through the front window of the helicopter and, framed between the pilot and the burn boss, I saw columns of smoke that outlined the perimeter of our project area. Firefighters on the ground had lit small fires to help us see the edges. As we did a test flight around the 432-acre burn, I could see my coworkers in yellow on the ground, working the firelines beyond the edges of the burn area.

After we did a dry run to pick out a good flight path, we turned on the PSD machine and started dropping balls. The air was so cold that it made my eyes tear up. I had to straddle the machine, which forced my right knee to be positioned outside the helicopter, directly in the driving wind. I also had to keep my head outside the helicopter in order to see where the balls were landing.

Despite the temperature, I had to stay focused on my job. It's too easy for balls to get jammed and catch on fire in the machine. There is a button that we use to shoot water inside the machine from a reservoir tank if that happens. Gratefully, on the Cabin Meadow burn, I was able to put out the small internal fires and complete a successful mission. But I'll always remember the struggle to keep warm in the midst of a fire!

As I shivered in the helicopter that day, I was reminded of a flight a few years earlier. That time I wasn't igniting a fire. I was just observing one—several, actually. You see, we don't put out every fire we detect in the parks. Some lightning-caused fires are allowed to spread because they actually improve forest health. In these cases, we do reconnaissance flights every few days to chart the fire's activity. If fires are very active, we may assign specially trained fire monitors to document the fire's movement on the ground.

One day, after the first significant snowfall of the season, I was sent on a recon flight in the backcountry to check the natural fires we knew about and to scout for any new ones. I remember the flight as magical and beautiful. All of the high peaks were frosted,

Fire!

Sequoia National Park

some of the lakes were starting to freeze and the smaller creeks looked like silver ribbons threading through the snow.

There had been lightning with the snowstorm and, in our check of all the small fires, we came upon a foxtail pine that was burning at over 9,000 feet on the Boreal Plateau. The tree was completely surrounded by snow and yet the fire was burning intensely. I knew that the next day there would be little evidence of that fire other than a blackened stump hole. If we hadn't flown over it when we did, no one would ever have seen it. That flight gave me a glimpse of something that most people rarely see and helped me to remember just how much of our parks do indeed remain wild.

I like recalling those cold days because it reminds me that fire sometimes defies people's assumptions. It can be destructive and chaotic, but also beneficial, methodical and beautiful. And yes, it can be cold, too. So I'll be sure to keep my layers ready.

Fire in the Swamp

by Bob Panko

It was a fine February morning as we set out leading a school field trip into the piney woods of Long Pine Key in Everglades National Park. It had been a damp February, so even though the sun was shining, a few mosquitoes settled onto their meal targets whenever we stopped in the shade. Their targets that day were the exposed arms and legs of a group of 12-year-old elementary school children from Massachusetts.

After we hiked for a while, Rick and I stopped and gathered the group. Rick is the fire ecologist on the Everglades fire management staff and was born and raised in south Florida. I am the fire management officer, a transplant originally from New Jersey who adopted the Everglades as a second home.

"Why do you think we brought you here?" I asked. The kids looked around and one said it sure seemed pretty. Another remarked that when the trip was planned they never thought they would be walking through a pine woods. He thought the Everglades was just a big swamp.

"We brought you here," I said, "because you all studied about the Everglades before you came on this trip. You know that this is the only place of its kind on earth. Right?"

An enthusiastic chorus of "Yes!" greeted my question.

"You all know that the Everglades is in danger of disappearing if we don't take care of it. This little section right here is probably the most unusual portion of the park. We're standing in what's left of a pine and prairie ecosystem that used to be much larger. About 98% of that ecosystem is gone now—cut down, plowed under and turned into cities and towns. This is one of the few places where it remains on earth. It is also a wonderful place to tell the story of the Everglades."

Rick stepped up to remind the kids of what we had discussed in our safety briefing prior to the start of our hike. "To keep out of harms way," he emphasized, "don't poke your hands into places that might be a hiding place for a rattlesnake or coral snake. Be mindful of where you stand or you might wind up in a nest of fire ants. Be careful not to brush against the number one source of injury to Everglades firefighters—the Florida poisonwood tree, which can be found throughout the Pinelands and can cause a bad rash just like the one you can get by touching poison oak or poison ivy."

Those last few warnings certainly got their attention. Snakes, biting ants and poison plants—a 12-year-old's dream!

Rick then asked them, "What forces of nature do you think formed this place?" The kids looked for clues. Right around us there was black char on the bark of living pine trees, silver trunks of pines that had been snapped during the fury of hurricane Andrew almost 15 years earlier and pines that had been more recently toppled by hurricanes Katrina and Wilma. There were also grasses and herbaceous plants all around us as diverse as a tropical rain forest.

With the cleverness of youth, one of them said, "It looks like a lot has happened here."

I smiled and said, "Indeed it has." I held up my hand with outstretched fingers. "There are five natural forces that shaped the Everglades. Who can tell me one?" One girl, having studied for her school field trip, stated that the Everglades needed more water. Another remarked that hurricanes did a lot of damage. Another thought that fire might be a factor. Given the amount of swatting going on, a few kids proposed that mosquitoes should be counted as a force of nature.

I stood back and told my story. "The five natural factors that shaped the Everglades are floods, drought, hurricanes, frost and fire." Water is the thing that everyone hears most about. There often seems to be too much or not enough. However, the ebb and flow of flood and drought are two vital parts of the Everglades ecosystem. The winters are always dry and the summers are always wet, which is as nature intended. There are vast parts of the Everglades that need to be dry in the winter and wet in the summer. This annual cycle of wet and dry is affected by larger climate impacts, like El Nino (which brings south Florida a wet, cool cycle) and La Nina (which brings a dry, warm cycle).

Regarding hurricanes—the third natural force on my list—I asked the question,

Fire!

Everglades National Park

"What is the biggest natural impact of hurricanes?" The children were quick to point to fallen trees nearby. Indeed, some trees did not withstand the storms; however, the pine trees where we stood had very small tops and almost no limbs on their trunks. They were adapted to hurricanes like a sailboat in a storm—not much sail up on the mast to catch the wind. Actually, very few of them died as a result of hurricanes.

"The most significant impact of hurricanes," I said, "is that they bring tropical plants and animals to the peninsula of Florida from throughout the Caribbean and as far away as Africa. Some of the plants and animals, which we call 'exotics,' crowd out the native species and take over areas of the Everglades."

The fourth natural force (which no one guessed) is frost. I went on to explain that every five to ten years a hard frost settles on the Everglades. In fact, one memorable day in January 1978, I awoke to find frost on the windshield of my car! Many of the tropical plants that had been there for years died because of the frost. The frost determines how far north these tropical plants and animals can exist on this thin Florida peninsula.

That left me to discuss the fifth natural force: fire. "Summer thunderstorms have always caused fires in the Everglades. The biggest ones happen early in the summer before the Everglades fills up with water. Most are small and get put out by rain from the same lightning storms that started them. Few plants or animals here would survive unless they had adapted to the dangers of naturally occurring fires. Remember how we talked about the way these pine trees had adapted to save themselves from hurricanes? Well, they've also adapted to protect themselves from fire. For example, you can see that they have very thick bark, an open canopy and very few low branches, so fire has a harder time igniting the trees. This strategy works because the wind pushes the flames away before there is enough heat to harm the tree. On the charred ground underneath the trees, seeds fall upon the nutrient-rich ashes left behind by the fire.

As managers of the land, we have made many efforts to control the natural forces of flood and drought. For many years we thought it would be smart to drain the Everglades. We have learned that the wetlands are important to the wel-being of not only the plants and animals, but also us humans. So we have worked to correct the mistakes of the past. We must always be mindful of the natural cycles of wet and dry weather. Hurricanes and frost are up to Mother Nature, but we can influence fire. The proper management of fire is one of the most important things we can do to help preserve the Everglades.

We combat winter fires that are caused by humans and that could damage the Everglades. Due to development outside the park, there are fewer naturally occurring fires in the late spring or early summer. Those summer fires are very good for the Everglades. They clear away the underbrush and give the bigger trees a better chance to survive. It might seem strange, but our most effective tool to care for the Everglades is to carefully set fires on purpose. These fires are called "prescribed burns."

To determine where and when to start a prescribed burn, we first look at what places in the Everglades lack the natural rhythm of fire. We work closely with the park scientists and create a plan that describes what we are trying to do and where and when the fire will burn. We figure out how many people we'll need to have on the ground to make sure the fire stays within the prescribed area. Then we go out and start the fire. Sometimes we even use a machine in a helicopter to help light the fire.

In the Everglades, we started doing prescribed burns way back in 1958. At that time, fires were generally considered to be a bad thing. Back then, all over America, when a fire started, people thought that the best thing to do was to put it out! Today, we all know more about the important role that fire plays in shaping the natural environment. Fire is one of Mother Nature's tools that keep the environment healthy. Now you all know the important role that fire plays in the Everglades, along with four other important forces of nature. Will you all do your best to learn more about how to protect the environment?"

Again, I heard a resounding "Yes!" and with that, we all decided it was time to move on and explore more of the pine woods of Everglades National Park.

The Trapper Fire

by Michael Ober

It was a typical Wednesday at Glacier National Park and I was working the 4 p.m. to midnight shift. The only thing that differed from any normal shift was that I picked up a ride-a-long partner. Angie, a fellow law enforcement ranger at Bowman Lake, was down from the North Fork District for eight hours of road patrol duty. We went through the usual routine—got the patrol car, checked the lights, radio, trunk gear, each other's gear, loaded the shotgun, prepared the shift report and headed up to Logan Pass from Apgar Village. We could see relentless columns of smoke from the Wedge and Trapper Fires, which were naturally caused by lightening strikes. These fires were allowed to burn for weeks, while rangers carefully observed their courses to ensure that they would not create a hazard for park visitors. The evening was calm, the sky clear and there was a typical amount of summer traffic. Angie and I settled into easy conversation, catching up on each other's summer events.

By the time we reached the Loop, part way up the Going-to-the-Sun Road to Logan Pass, it was clear that something was not right with the Trapper Fire. It felt angry and restless to me, like it was bracing for some kind of noteworthy run after slowly chewing up ground fuels for days. Whole groups of trees were beginning to torch and

 huge black clouds of smoke were rising from Upper McDonald Valley. Visibility was deteriorating rapidly. What had once been a remote natural fire had now crept into the valley and had begun to pose a public safety threat. Its status changed immediately to "suppression." The communications center called to inform us that the Trapper Fire incident commander had declared that the road should be closed immediately because of imminent runs near the

BILL BACHMAN

Glacier National Park

Loop. We began working with other patrol units to shut the road down. The gate at Big Bend on the east side was closed, along with the west gate at Avalanche. Angie and I, in our vehicle, and our supervisor, Gary, in his vehicle, started a sweep, looking for cars in between the gates, sending them east or west to clear the road in the path of the fire. We'd done this before and knew the routine.

Then came an unexpected twist. Folks we had sent down the road from above the Loop came back to our position at Crystal Point and, with wide eyes and incredulous looks, told us that they couldn't get through because the fire was right next to the Loop! We were sure that this couldn't be happening. We had just been there and, while there was a lot of smoke, the passage appeared safe for visitors. Angie and I quickly drove toward the Loop. It took only a few curves in the road and less than a quarter of a mile before we recognized that something was terribly wrong with the Trapper Fire. Worse, we were trapped above the Loop with no way down. Several cars full of east-bound visitors emerged from the wall of smoke and whizzed by us. They flashed their lights and shook their heads with the silent message "you don't want to go down there." Meanwhile, our radio was bursting with traffic. Swiftcurrent Lookout reported that the area was engulfed in thick, dark smoke and that just before the view was obscured, the fire was seen making a run uphill from Mineral Creek. Maintenance personnel at Granite Park Chalet radioed that they were trying desperately to collect hikers and guests at the chalet and had started the pumps for structural fire protection.

Meanwhile, Gary, who was below us at the west tunnel, radioed that he was inching his way up to the Loop to see if he could get through. Angie and I were stopped in the middle of the road when, moments later, Gary's Ford Expedition emerged from the black and orange inferno that had swallowed up the entire Loop area. "It's not too bad," he reported, "I think we can make it back down." We rolled up the windows, Angie shifted into gear and we followed him cautiously downhill into the fire zone.

We were all concerned about accounting for the people and vehicles at the Loop. We had to be certain that everyone was evacuated and away from the threat. Gary radioed that there were two vehicles remaining but he could not locate the occupants. There was also a lone bicycle resting against the rock wall in the upper parking lot. If the people who owned the vehicles were hiking on the Loop Trail in the path of the fire—well, there was simply nothing that any of us could do.

When we arrived at the Loop it was eerily dark. Fire was burning on both sides of the road, licking at everything combustible with a hungry crackle. Short canopy runs were erupting both below and above the parking lot; brush and ground fuels were burning steadily, and burning branches, large and small, were falling all around. Debris was everywhere and layers of burned pine needles littered the surface like millions of fallen soldiers.

Jumping out of an air-conditioned patrol vehicle into such a scene is to be completely engulfed in the overpowering heat. Heat poured off the road surface, the nearby rocks and even the trees themselves, which were pulsing flames and shooting hot air everywhere. Gary stopped and raced toward the bicycle. I followed and we threw the bike into the back of his vehicle. I jumped back in the patrol car and Angie followed Gary around the swirling arc of the Loop. As Gary had said, there were two cars left in the parking lots, but they were locked and there was no time to save them, no time to linger. The Trapper Fire was exploding around us.

As we sped by the second vehicle, I noticed that it had Idaho plates and it struck Angie and me at the same moment—"Wait...! That one belongs to Chris." She's the Swiftcurrent fire lookout. I got on the radio and called her. "Chris, I need to know exactly where your keys are. There's no time." She knew what I meant and described the hiding place for her spare keys. I sprang from the air-conditioned car into the heat again and told Angie to get turned downhill in preparation for a quick exit. Frantically, I searched for the keys and with them finally in-hand, I raced to the door, unlocked the car, started it up and shoved the pedal down. Nothing. OH NO! Wait. I forgot about the parking brake! Where's the release? Look! Look! Ah, got it! I roared out of there and swung in behind the waiting patrol vehicle. "Go Angie," I whispered. Then out loud I bellowed, "GO ANGIE!" But she'd already gone, streaking downhill from the fire zone. She soon emerged into the cool clear daylight of the highway near the west tunnel. As I accelerated away from heat and fire of the lower parking lot, I glanced out of the window to see two of the portable potties on fire and a third one that had melted and collapsed into a molten heap of bubbling, smoking green-gray plastic. Fortunately, no one was hurt that day and I even ended up receiving a really nice bottle of red wine as a thank you gift from Chris. It was just another normal day in the life of a ranger at Glacier National Park, where you never know what surprises will come tomorrow.

The Lookout Tower

by Franklin Clark

I hadn't seen the lookout tower at Schonchin Butte since leaving Lava Beds National Monument a decade ago. This trip would be special. It would be my first time back since Gary, my mentor and the former chief of interpretation, passed away. Printed on his funeral prayer book was the quote, "You never really leave a place you love. You take a part of it with you and leave a part of yourself behind." I agree with this sentiment and believe that by visiting Lava Beds, in some small way I will be visiting Gary.

I chained my bike to the trailhead sign and noticed the absence of the United States flag above the lookout tower. Yesterday, thunderstorms skirted the monument. I hoped that Ranger George, whom I saw at the visitor center, would tell someone I was visiting, especially if lightning seemed imminent. I imagined park rangers inviting me to once again staff the lookout tower while ominous clouds shot toward the stratosphere.

Wishful thinking! I scolded myself. You can't go backwards and relive your glory days. This was a farewell visit, a time to come to terms with change. It was a time to reconnect to the Modoc Spirits, to try to feel Gary's presence, and to say goodbye to Schonchin and Lava Beds.

On the steep climb up—the equivalent of 50 flights of stairs—I took my time 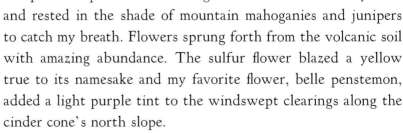 and rested in the shade of mountain mahoganies and junipers to catch my breath. Flowers sprung forth from the volcanic soil with amazing abundance. The sulfur flower blazed a yellow true to its namesake and my favorite flower, belle penstemon, added a light purple tint to the windswept clearings along the cinder cone's north slope.

After signing the trail register at Schonchin's summit, I

Fire!

Lava Beds National Monument

bounded up the steps to the lookout's catwalk. A moment later, the door opened and out stepped a woman. She said hello and I returned her greeting. Her ranger uniform had sharp creases and looked new. I glanced at her name tag, which read "Courtney." We chatted and I explained that I was up to take some photos. She invited me in for a tour and as I stepped through the door, I saw a familiar photo above the desk.

"I'm glad my picture is still here," I remarked.

"You used to work here?" Courtney asked.

"Yeah. Back in the 90s."

"Really? What's your name?"

"Frank Clark. I wrote my name on the back of the photo," I said pointing to the framed eight-by- ten.

Courtney pulled down the frame, flipped it over and found my name with a date. She flipped it again and studied the image. The picture was a black silhouette of me standing on the lookout's edge, the outline of binoculars held to my eyes, with the red, white and blue of the American flag waving overhead. There were tall clouds with puffy white tops and flat, dark-blue bottoms that day, looming menacingly in the background of the picture.

"Ken, my fire management officer, took that just before the storm of the decade. I called in dozens of smoke sightings in just a few days. In fact, that was my first day alone in the tower." How quickly 11 years had passed; it seemed like yesterday that Ken snapped the photo. My eyes lost focus as my thoughts drifted back in time.

* * *

Ken put his camera away, waved goodbye and disappeared behind a juniper. I was alone. I scanned the horizon for smoke, pausing occasionally to monitor the fast-building clouds. Ken expected a massive storm. I couldn't imagine storms disturbing the serene environment. The last three days, while in training, I'd come to consider Schonchin a silent and bright refuge from fire fighting. That image was about to be smashed forever.

Within an hour of Ken's departure, storm clouds began to form southeast of the monument. I grew increasingly nervous and paced around the catwalk looking skyward. Suddenly dozens of flashes lit up the sky, followed shortly by violent thunder. It seemed as if the blast might rattle the windows loose. My eyes grew wide and my knees trembled. I stumbled inside to mark the locations of the lightning strikes on the Osborne Fire Finder map—a device used by fire lookouts to find a directional bearing (azimuth) of smoke. I then radioed the information to Modoc National Forest dispatch.

* * *

Courtney replaced the photo, her movement jarring me back to the present. My eyes fixed on the fire finder. I approached the stand, looked at the stenciled numbers on the map and had the overwhelming feeling that I had just been using it yesterday. On the fire finder's pedestal hung a clipboard with fire reports. I bent down for a closer look. My mind wandered back as I remembered how jittery my hands were the first time I filled out a report.

* * *

I mustered all my courage, steadied my voice and reported the lightning strikes. Moments later there were more strikes and soon a grey plume danced toward the sky. I rushed to the spotting scope. Flames burst from a lone juniper and quickly spread to dry sage. I hurried to the fire finder, aligned its crosshair through the base of the fire and looked at the azimuth indicator. My shaking hands fumbled for the fire reports hanging from the pedestal. I hurriedly scribbled information: azimuth, size, distance, location and fuel type. Seconds later, I radioed Modoc and successfully reported my first smoke sightings.

* * *

A high-pitched tone on the radio woke me from my daydreams. Courtney recorded the forecast and I looked toward Mt. Shasta as the clouds began to build and darken. Returning to the catwalk, I packed my backpack as if leaving, but Courtney asked me questions about the rapidly developing clouds. I spent half an hour eating lunch and going over weather and scanning techniques with Courtney. Just as I was packing up, a single slender bolt of lightning split the sky in the distance.

"Did you see that?" Courtney shook her head. "You've gotta get an azimuth on it!"

We rushed inside and I helped Courtney record the strike. Another strike flashed only yards from the lookout and I had to shut the window, as nickel-sized hail and rain pelted the ledge. I could tell from Courtney's appreciative comments that she was glad to have company. I remembered my first day alone as the lookout and smiled. I knew exactly how she felt.

* * *

It was midnight and, after hours alone, Ken instructed me to shut down the lookout and head down the hill. I had survived lightning strikes near the tower, reported a dozen smoke sightings, guided the engine crew to the largest fire, and had done so calmly and effectively. I felt like I'd found my home atop Schonchin Butte. Over the next few days, the fire crew, who had generally regarded my frail frame with disdain, greeted me warmly and appreciatively. Ken told me I had earned their respect. I had weathered the storm.

* * *

"You can weather any storm, Courtney. You'll do just fine this summer."

At her request, I helped with procedures for the next hour as we hunkered down during the storm. Then the sun split the clouds and the rain stopped as abruptly as it had begun. I stepped outside and took a deep breath of the fragrant mountain air, cleansed by the heavy rain. It was a smell that set my soul at ease. A beautiful rainbow appeared over the horizon, reaching north from the Schonchin Butte parking lot to Symbol Bridge in the south. My eyes welled up, and I felt a presence in the air.

"Courtney, you have to see this," I whispered in awe.

Joining me, she gasped.

"I've experienced many beautiful days on Schonchin, but I've never seen anything like this. It's so close and full, and it ends at Symbol Bridge, a sacred site where the Modocs painted pictographs."

"That must be a metaphor. It must mean something."

"Gary." I whispered. "The Spirits."

"What's that?"

"Yes. It must mean something," I repeated.

That evening, I sat in the utter silence, basking in the moonlight among the junipers and sage. At the end of a long first day back—after the storm, after the sightings, after the rainbow, after hugging Courtney goodbye—I felt that everything was now as it should be. The Spirits and Gary had returned to show me amazing beauty and love. I cried for Gary and for all the wonderful people I had met over the last decade but would never see again. I cried for all the tremendous beauty in the world. Finally, after a decade of wandering, I had returned home.

Fire!

Forces of Nature

Makule - The Old One
- HAWAI'I VOLCANOES NATIONAL PARK -

Hurricane Survival on the Outer Banks
- CAPE HATTERAS NATIONAL SEASHORE -

Flash Flood in the Driest Spot in America
- DEATH VALLEY NATIONAL PARK -

Haberdeventure, A Dwelling Place in the Winds
- THOMAS STONE NATIONAL HISTORIC SITE -

Packs Antelope
- MOUNT RUSHMORE NATIONAL MEMORIAL -
&
- BADLANDS NATIONAL PARK -

Over the course of millennia, national park wilderness areas have evolved to exhibit some of the most breathtaking scenery on the planet. Extraordinary forces of nature have helped to create these special places, which have been set aside for people to visit, learn from, preserve and enjoy. While most often cherished for their peace and tranquility, it's fun and enlightening to learn about the prehistoric, historic and ongoing events that helped shape our parks.

Continuing geologic change is evident in all natural settings. It's there to be seen in recent rockslides or, more subtly, in slowly rising or lowering elevations. There is also paleontological evidence: Dinosaur tracks and bones are found in a number of parks, providing prehistoric images of another time. Skeletons of ancient species of fish and reptiles are found in rocks far from any known water source. Fossilized plants teach us about life on the planet long ago. Opportunities to learn are everywhere in the parks.

Millions of years ago extreme weather and dramatic geological events shaped some of these fantastic landscapes. Mountains rose slowly when tectonic plates shifted in massive earthquakes. This lifted the land vertically, forming the Rocky Mountain, Sierra Nevada and Appalachian Ranges, among others. Other spectacular peaks, such as Lassen and the Cascade Range, were formed volcanically.

Geologic forces are still active and visible today. Mauna Loa and Kilauea volcanoes in Hawai'i Volcanoes National Park are two of the world's most dynamic. Lava flows add new land to the park each year. Yellowstone provides a present-day look at a primordial landscape, with bubbling mud pots, geysers, fumaroles and hot springs fueled by heat from the molten rock of a "super volcano" located below the earth's surface. A large section of Yellowstone is contained within a giant caldera, measuring as much as 45 miles across. Imagine the devastating impact on the landscape when a volcano of this size erupts, which it last did approximately 640,000 years ago, spreading a thick layer of volcanic ash over the majority of North America!

Unlike volcanoes and earthquakes, other forces can be far more gradual, such as erosion by water, glacial ice and wind. These natural forces continue to shape the landscape slowly but relentlessly. The Grand Canyon was carved inch-by-inch by water flowing over rock for millions of years. Glaciers formed Yosemite Valley and many other exquisite scenes, moving at an almost imperceptible pace. They scooped away the land, creating deep valleys, polishing stone and leaving behind occasional boulders scattered across the landscape as reminders of their passing.

People tend to think of geologic events as a part of the ancient past, but geologic changes continue today. Some are fast and dramatic. Rockslides change the faces of cliffs and canyons, and, together with avalanches, have destroyed many roads in national parks. Earthquakes, hurricanes, tornadoes, avalanches, cyclones, tsunamis and wildfires have all dramatically impacted and forever changed our world. Floods can change whole landscapes and have washed away entire campgrounds and even moved buildings from their foundations. In Death Valley, a flash flood swept cars as far as a mile from where they were parked, filling them with dirt and rocks and pushing them along like tumbleweeds in a desert breeze. Park managers ideally allow land affected by natural forces to recover over time; however, natural disasters often require extraordinarily costly repairs to keep our parks accessible for the public to enjoy.

In 2005, Hurricane Katrina and several others caused catastrophic damage along the Atlantic and Gulf coasts. The storms severely damaged many National Park Service sites, including Everglades, Dry Tortugas and Biscayne National Parks; Big Cypress and Big Thicket National Preserves; Cape Lookout, Gulf Islands and Canaveral National Seashores; and Jean Lafitte and New Orleans Jazz National Historical Parks. The storms caused incalculable human suffering, yet were mere blips when viewed on a geologic timeline of events that have shaped our planet.

Nature's astonishing strength and patience has created amazing places that are protected as national parks. Mother Nature humbles us, proving how helpless we are in the face of her fury. At the same time, forces of nature can be a source of inspiration. In many native cultures, nature's powers play a significant role in tribal belief systems. Many native stories reflect a spiritual connection to the forces that shaped our world.

American Indians in the Cascade Range of Oregon witnessed Mount Mazama's destruction, forming Crater Lake. This volcano literally blew its top and collapsed. Oral traditions explain this cataclysm based on the power of the spirit-god Llao. To this day Native Hawaiians make offerings to Pele, the goddess of volcanoes, who settled in the crater of Halema'uma'u on the summit of Kilauea Volcano in Hawai'i Volcanoes National Park. The lives and culture of Native Alaskans, such as the Inupiat, are also closely linked to forces of nature, especially those influenced by man. Global warming has begun to impact costal villages and is a threat to their traditional lifestyle. The Inupiat people rely heavily on subsistence hunting and fishing, and the thinning sea ice has reduced access to many of their food sources. It has also contributed to coastal flooding and erosion.

By studying the natural forces that shaped our parks, we can learn more about how they continue to impact our planet. Hopefully this knowledge will teach us to appreciate and preserve the natural balance of the delicate ecosystem we call home.

Makule - The Old One

by Carol Kracht

The afternoon promised to be baking hot and dry. Wispy cirrus clouds curved through the sky above Ka'aha, a coastal backcountry camping shelter on the island of Hawai'i. This was a resupply pack trip for the trail crew, a job for me, a mule wrangler at Hawai'i Volcanoes National Park, along with two of my four-legged crew. Fresh from Oregon, I was just beginning to find my way around in my new position.

I unloaded my pack mule, Makule, meaning "old one" in Hawaiian. He is a creamy golden Belgian cross mule with a corner missing out of one long velvety ear and plenty of attitude. I longed to stay at Ka'aha, gazing out at the deep blue sea glittering with reflected sun and listening to the waves crashing on the black pahoehoe shore. (Pahoehoe is hardened lava with a smooth, ropy surface.) Pockets of salt and pepper sand, mingled with tide pools, beckoned me to kick off my riding boots, roll up my green National Park Service pants and wiggle my toes in their gritty heat and luxurious coolness. However, my watch sternly reminded me that we needed to get back. Ahead lay three and a half miles of trail, including the treacherous Hilina Pali, a steep cliff, rising 2,283 feet up from sea level in a two-mile ride. This section resembled a ladder of jumbled rock more than a riding trail.

I mounted my sorrel mare Lio, which means "horse" in Hawaiian, and turned toward the pali (cliff), leading Makule behind us with his empty sawbuck packsaddle. Both Lio and Makule plodded along reluctantly under the Hawaiian sun, no more eager than I to tackle the tough climb back. The first mile wanders between rolling ropey sections of black pahoehoe lava and tufts of sun-baked blades of pili grass. Makule was an expert

G. BRAD LEWIS

Hawai'i Volcanoes National Park

at snatching mouthfuls on the move. Grass to go. Lio moved on listlessly, slower than usual, seemingly half asleep. Then, the quick movement of a mongoose startled her into wakefulness and a full-blown jump to the side. I felt her falter once, twice, slip, then regain her footing on the rock. But four steps later I knew she had bruised her sole. She was limping and now stood unevenly, favoring one hoof. There was no choice but to dismount. The prospect of hiking up Hilina Pali in riding boots was disheartening. Staring up at the rocky cliff before me I decided to go to Plan B. Now was a good time to see if Makule was indeed "broke to ride." I had heard from the trail crew that he was, but I hadn't seen it for myself. In my world, horses were ridden and mules were packed. I began switching tack. Lio's trail saddle fit Makule and the cinch could be adjusted. The bridle, however, was hopeless. Makule's big muley head was, well, just too big to get a fit. No worries, a halter with a looped lead rope would have to do. After all, on this trail the only choice was up. Lio would carry the empty sawbuck, relieving her of weight on that now tender front hoof.

I patted Makule, assuring him that my 125 pounds would be nothing in comparison to his usual loads of 180 pounds. Setting my left foot in the stirrup I cautiously mounted up. He stood completely still, then slowly turned his head to look sideways at me, as if to say, "What do you think you're doing up there?" Well, it was a better first reaction than a buck. I held Lio's lead rope and urged Makule forward. He immediately disagreed. He knew that his job was to be behind the horse—definitely not in front. As I coaxed him forward, with only a halter for front-end control, he began to turn in circles in his attempt to get behind Lio, which was his idea of the correct position. For a few moments we were just a tangle of rope in a merry-go-round before I managed to get Makule pointed in the right direction up the trail. It took a lot of coaxing, clucking and prodding to keep him moving as we began the climb up the pali.

Horses and mules each have a different way of looking at the world. In my experience the horse asks, "How do you want something done?" Whereas the mule asks, "WHY?" You better have the right answer or he will just as likely quit on you as obey you. Makule was definitely asking WHY at each step up. "Why do I have to be in the lead? Why are you sitting on me? Why do I have to climb back up this blasted trail?!" Still, I somehow managed to convince him that it would all be worth his while. There were promises of water, alfalfa cubes, carrots and a trailer ride back to the pasture once we reached the top.

Then, abruptly, he stopped dead in his tracks. We were about halfway. To our right, there was a rock wall face. To our left there was only a sheer drop. He refused to take another step. No amount of clucking, kicking or coaxing was apparently going to change his muley mind. That was when I decided to go to Plan C. (Mule packers must always be open to a change of plans.) I would have to dismount and hike the rest of the way in my riding boots, leading my recalcitrant mule and gimpy mare. As I shifted my weight to dismount, painfully aware that the two-foot-wide trail left little room for me to perch on, Makule shifted left, leaving me a mere two inches to step down on. "Fine time to move," I grumbled, trying to encourage him back over a bit to the right against the rock wall. No dice! He simply turned his head back toward my knee and pushed me up with his muzzle, then swung his head back facing forward. Great, so now he was getting pushy about me getting off. He stood stock-still, ears pricked forward in rapt attention, alert in statuesque form. At the same moment Lio pulled back, yanking the lead rope taut between us.

I turned in my saddle to look back at her foolishness and it was as if a wave of ice water swept through my veins. Countless lines of solidified, broken lava rock were streaming down the cliff behind us like waterfalls. Ahead was a mirror image of the same. You might think that tons of falling rock would sound like a freight train but all I remember was silence. All earthly sounds were extinguished and time stood still. It must have been a fear-induced trick of my mind that suddenly made the world seem utterly silent. The rockslide seemed to last forever; however, in reality, it probably lasted about ten minutes. Perhaps the mind slows things down as a protective mechanism to give a person time to react in the face of danger?

The realization of what was happening had me swallowing the bitter metallic taste of fear. Pele, the goddess of Kilauea, had spoken. The earth shuddered violently beneath the volcano. I dared not look up, certain that a rockslide would crash down on us. I buried my face in Makule's warm neck, hugging him close to my heart for what seemed like an endless prayer. The rock wall to our right divided the spills to the front and rear of us, never touching a single hair on my mule, my horse or myself. Five meters forward or back and we surely would have been pushed from the trail and off the cliff.

Suddenly my radio crackled to life. Sound was restored. A barely audible dispatch informed us all about what was dangerously obvious to me, while perched on a two-foot trail halfway up Hilina Pali. Earthquake! Later we learned that the earthquake measured 5.5 on the Richter scale.

As abruptly as it had begun, it was over. The pali settled back to reality. I wondered if our trail was blocked. Makule shifted his weight, then dropped his head to snatch a lone tuft of sun-bleached grass. Life was back to normal. He chewed thoughtfully for a moment, then began to move up the trail with Lio following. Makule had sensed the earthquake. By fortune or grace he had stopped on the safest possible section of trail. Stroking his golden neck as he lunged up the next bank of rock I realized that, if I was going to survive in this new land of lava, volcanoes and earthquakes, I had better take the time to listen to my coworkers. Especially the ones with long velvety ears.

Hurricane Survival
on the Outer Banks

by Kenny Ballance

My home is on Ocracoke Island on the southernmost tip of the chain that makes up Cape Hatteras National Seashore on the Outer Banks of North Carolina. The island is approximately 17 miles long, three miles wide, and is only accessible by private boat, ferry or plane. Since 1789, eleven generations of my family have lived on this windswept island, which is best known as the place where the pirate Blackbeard once roamed. Ocracoke Island is also known for its rich and colorful history, wild ponies, British Cemetery, breathtaking natural beaches, and the oldest operating lighthouse on National Park Service (NPS) property. It was built in 1823! These and many other attractions keep visitors coming back each year to Ocracoke.

Ninety percent of Ocracoke Island is managed by the NPS. Private individuals own the remaining ten percent of the island, which is contained within the Ocracoke Village. Many locals are happy that the federal government manages the majority of the island. With NPS protection, the island has kept its quaint local character and charm, and, most of all, its pristine beaches. There are about 850 permanent local residents but, during the summer, the population soars to between 5,000 and 7,000 people. Small dirt paths and family cemeteries can be seen in the village. Familiar family names are very noticeable when talking to the island's residents, who speak with a distinct local brogue.

From the time I was a small child, I heard numerous storm survival stories that were a normal part of life on the island. Park rangers always played an important role in these stories, especially in communications, law enforcement and the daily monitoring of life-threatening weather situations. Hurricanes, nor'easters and being completely cut off from the mainland are constant threats

188

here on Ocracoke Island.

In the early years of my career as a park ranger in the mid-1970s, communications were limited to an inadequate radio system, three television stations and very poor radio channels. There were no cell phones or Internet back then. Information on deteriorating weather conditions was passed to residents by the U.S. Coast Guard. There was no medical facility on the island and the nearest hospital was 170 miles away in Elizabeth City. Park rangers were trained as emergency medical technicians and worked with the Ocracoke Voluntary Rescue and Fire Department. The ranger station was always the emergency operation center.

In 1985, as Hurricane Gloria approached, local agencies—the NPS, ferry division, Coast Guard, Sheriff's Department, marine fisheries, local power company and volunteer fire department—worked together preparing the village residents and tourists for evacuation. After closing the campgrounds and motels, tourists were encouraged to evacuate, although there wasn't a mandatory evacuation policy in effect. Visitors and residents were told that once ferry service was discontinued, there would be no way off the island. This was one of the many times when I stayed behind on Ocracoke Island to help during a hurricane.

Local residents prepared for the storm the way they have for centuries. Preparations included filling kerosene lanterns, stocking up on candles, storing nonperishable food, boarding up windows and cutting holes in the floors of houses so that they wouldn't float off their foundations. Fresh water was drawn from cisterns that were then refilled with water so they wouldn't float away.

Local fishermen secured their boats using extra moorings or tied them to trees. Residents secured their small animals, and horses and cattle were turned loose to find higher ground. Park service horses were put in higher elevation areas of the corrals. During Hurricane Gloria, I stayed at the Crews Inn Bed and Breakfast with my two childhood nannies, Mildred and Muzel, who were in their 90s. Since the inn had survived many storms, I felt that it was the best place to be. The three-story building was built with lumber from shipwrecks that had washed up on the beach, a common practice in earlier years. Just before Gloria made landfall, several evacuating residents brought their animals to spend the storm with us. The animals included cats, dogs, goats, six chickens and one rooster, whose displacement resulted in lots of off-schedule

LAURENCE PARENT

Cape Hatteras National Seashore

crowing. Between the animals barking, meowing, baaing and crowing, and the constant information requests from the media (CBS, NBC, local newspapers), there was much activity at the Crews Inn Bed and Breakfast.

The park provided safe harbor for fishing trawlers and other vessels at the Ocracoke docks. As in other big storms, as many as 50 vessels sought safe harbor at the docks. All types of park rangers worked together securing facilities, evacuating visitors and securing the Ocracoke ponies. While preparing for the storm, employees from all the agencies were fed at the Coast Guard station, and residents were invited to ride out the storm there, too. Park staff monitored beach and highway conditions, and went door-to-door to offer weather forecast information. If conditions during the storm became too dangerous to stay at their homes, essential personnel could go to the Coast Guard station or to the lighthouse keeper's quarters.

As the storm raged, old and new houses creaked and moaned. The wind pounded the timbers and lumber that held the houses together. Trees fell, power lines snapped and debris was blown everywhere. Locals constantly looked out the windows, waiting for the storm surge. They knew that if the storm surge approached from the sound side, those living on the back of the island would hear it coming. When it did come, water was suddenly everywhere. From their houses, locals monitored how high the water was rising. "It's up to the first step," someone yelled. "It's now on the third step," someone else hollered.

When water seeped onto the porch and then pooled under the front door of the inn, everyone rushed to grab furniture and belongings and move them to the second floor. People with one-story houses piled their belongings to the ceiling and waded around in their houses hoping the water would recede. Boats broke their moorings and people worried that the vessels would crash into their houses. Many boats were destroyed by the pounding waves and violent winds.

When the storm finally ended, the wind subsided and the water gradually receded. It was then that damage assessments could begin. My fellow rangers and I assisted local agencies in checking on elderly residents and those with medical conditions. Residents checked on their neighbors, often using boats to access houses. The power was out, phone service was down, roads were inaccessible and the ferries were not running. Highway 12 was impassible between the village and campground. It was almost surreal, especially when I looked out the window and saw a Boston Whaler passing by on the flooded highway. Downed trees and power lines were everywhere; dead animals and debris were strewn about. Coffins had floated out of the ground. My sister saw two coffins from the local cemetery floating down the highway in front of her house. My father and I, along with a local friend, carried the coffins back to the cemetery so that the funeral home staff could rebury them when they were able to return from the mainland. Before reburial, I contacted the wife of one of the coffins' inhabitants. Her husband had been dead for seven years. She requested that his coffin be opened, his wedding ring removed and the ring returned to her. It was quite an emotional time.

Residents began cleaning up their houses, sweeping out mud, sand and debris. Dead fish were found under furniture. Residents were advised not to drink cistern water because of possible contamination. The NPS provided safe drinking water from the system at the visitor center. After all was secure in the village, rangers completed an assessment of the beach, side roads and airstrip. We also checked on the Ocracoke pony herd and facilities. Residents have often depended on park rangers for assistance and guidance during the severe storms and, as a part of the community, we were proud to serve them in both the preparation and recovery efforts necessitated by Hurricane Gloria.

Cape Hatteras National Seashore is still faced with approaching hurricanes and nor'easters. During these times of imminent disaster, the park initiates the incident command system, and the whole park staff works together to get the job done. With much more modern communication equipment, hurricane and storm response is more effective. Storm assignments have become normal operations and are taken in stride. There is something special about the way Cape Hatteras residents respect and care for one another. It makes me proud to be both a National Park Service ranger and a "banker."

Flash Flood in the Driest Spot in America

by Charlie Callagan

Imagine your worst nightmare. For me that nightmare is drowning. Would I stand right at the edge of a thousand-foot cliff? You bet! But, venture into water over my head? No way! I can't swim. Maybe that's why I live in Death Valley, the driest spot in the country with less than two inches of annual rainfall. On August 15, 2004 my worst nightmare nearly came true.

I've worked as a wilderness ranger in Olympic National Park and as a bear ranger in Glacier National Park. I thrive on adventure. I even have a reputation as a storm chaser. The excitement and allure of Mother Nature at her most extreme is just too much for me to ignore.

On that summer day in 2004, I had seen thunderheads building and dissipating all day. I was at home that evening when the sky began to look really ominous. Multiple lighting strikes lit up the southeastern horizon. Of course I just had to investigate, so off I went in my 4-wheel drive SUV, stopping by headquarters to pick up a radio "just in case." Running out the door, I waved to the superintendent and said, "I'm off to check out the storm." Knowing the potential danger of flash floods he urged me to use caution and to be safe. Fascinating as a flash flood may be, it's important to never drive across a flooded area.

Driving east past the Furnace Creek Inn, which was closed for the summer, my excitement grew as the first raindrops hit the windshield. When you live in the driest spot in the country, it doesn't take much rain to cause a thrill. My excitement quickly turned to amazement as I drove through the tight curves of lower Furnace Creek Wash. The rain was pounding down so hard that

MARC MUENCH

Death Valley National Park

my windshield wipers could hardly keep up. I couldn't remember ever being in rain this hard. At about that time, I noticed a light film of water flowing across the roadway.

Immediately my excitement turned into concern, as I realized that it wouldn't be long before a flash flood would head down the wash. Draining over 200 square miles, Furnace Creek Wash is bounded on the east by the rugged, sparsely vegetated Funeral Mountains and on the west by the easily eroded badlands. The wash has flooded many times over the decades. After particularly devastating floods in 1941, the owners of the Furnace Creek Inn decided to do something about it. Just upstream from Zabriskie Point they built a low divide to alter the course of floodwater and protect the Inn. Locally known as "the cut," it was engineered to capture the entire flow of upper Furnace Creek Wash and divert it through Gower Gulch.

Knowing that a flood was on its way, I tried to use my radio to send out a warning but the battery was dead. I had just decided to turn around and head for safety, when I noticed vehicle lights ahead. I knew that I had to warn the people, so I drove to the Zabriskie Point parking lot and pulled up next to two vans and a sedan. As I ran up to their windows, I quickly became soaked.

I'm a ranger naturalist here in Death Valley, but my old law enforcement training came in handy. I remembered to use a "voice of authority," but I couldn't have presented a very authoritative figure out of uniform and dripping wet. I went up to each vehicle, identified myself as an off-duty park ranger and briskly warned them that a flash flood was on its way. I insisted that under no circumstances should they continue east into the storm and recommended that they either stay put or follow me back to safety. There were German visitors in two of the vehicles and they seemed to understand what I was saying. I felt they would be OK if they stayed put but hoped they would follow me to a safer area. How wrong could I be!

Dashing back to my SUV, I wanted to get out of there before water from Echo Canyon began to flood the lower Furnace Creek Wash. I paused at the stop sign and honked my horn, but saw no movement and raced for home and safety. Boy was I in for a surprise! In the pitch dark and driving rain, I didn't realize that the flooding had begun. In my haste, I had actually driven directly into the floodwaters from Echo Canyon!

As I crossed the muddy water, it started pushing the vehicle off the road. I felt panic building and gunned the engine, fishtailing a bit before straightening out and moving quickly through the floodwater. With my heart in my throat and my adrenaline rushing, I realized that I was in a race for my life. What of the folks at Zabriskie Point? My heart sank and I was consumed with dread. If they had followed me, they wouldn't be able to cross the floodwater safely. Hopefully they stayed put and the cut would protect them. After all, it had successfully diverted the floodwater for sixty years!

As I entered the tight curves in the lower wash, I met a vehicle driving toward the oncoming flood. I have to admit that I really didn't want to slow down, as I was in survival mode, but how could I leave them to an uncertain fate?

Flipping on my emergency blinkers and flashing my headlights, I signaled them to stop. As we both rolled down our windows, I shouted, "There's a flood coming, turn around if you want to live!" and I was out of there. I turned another corner only to see yet another vehicle. I stopped them and repeated the same urgent warning and quickly continued on my way, not waiting to see if they heeded my advice.

I raced past the Inn ahead of the flood and sped to headquarters. I rushed past the superintendent and shouted that a flash flood was on its way down Furnace Creek Wash. Grabbing a radio, I notified emergency dispatch and requested they call the chief ranger.

I started to relax a bit, knowing that I'd had a close call, but was happy that I was able to get the emergency response in motion. Still, I couldn't sit around doing nothing, knowing that others might drive toward the approaching flood. With the fully charged radio in hand, I went back out into the storm. Even though I had known a flash flood was on its way, I was still shocked by what I saw. In less than ten minutes, the floodwater had arrived with a vengeance. It was several feet deep and was rushing past the Inn.

The chief ranger and others soon arrived. The excitement and urgency grew as vehicles began floating by, disappearing into the darkness. We later learned that the vehicles had belonged to resort employees and all were unoccupied. I didn't sleep well that night, as I was worried about the fate of the dozen visitors I had warned.

The next day was sunny and hot. Helicopters searched for survivors or victims, and we became aware of the full magnitude of the flood. Thirteen miles of Highway 190 were destroyed and 100 miles of park roads were closed because of flood debris. The park was shut down and all visitors were evacuated. Electricity was out and water and sewage lines were destroyed. Satellite photos showed how a strong, slow moving thunderstorm, centered over the Furnace Creek drainage, had dropped over two inches of rain in less than an hour, creating a flood of record proportions. For the first time since it was built, the Gower Gulch diversion was not able to absorb a flood. Scientists say that most of the floodwater overwhelmed the cut and flowed several feet deep across the Zabriskie Point parking lot. The force of the water floated two 20-ton concrete restrooms off their bases. The flood quickly moved downstream, joined Echo Canyon floodwater, then roared past the Inn to the bottom of Death Valley.

The news came that the three vehicles and all the passengers that I had warned by Zabriskie Point were stranded, but OK. They later recounted how they had been afraid for their lives as the floodwater rushed around them in the darkness. Their good fortune had stranded them on a high section of pavement near the parking lot, above the reach of floodwaters. We also received sad news. Two victims had been found in a pickup truck, the only flood deaths in the modern history of Death Valley, the driest spot in the country.

As unfortunate as those two deaths were, I felt tremendous relief that all of the visitors that I had contacted the night before had survived the flood.

Haberdeventure,
A Dwelling Place in the Winds

by Scott Hill

Most people have never heard of Thomas Stone and few know about his contributions to American history. Fewer still know about the site that has been set aside to remember him. The small 322-acre site is only 30 miles south of the metropolis of Washington, D.C. and yet can seem like a different world. As an interpretive ranger, I introduce visitors to this little-known patriot, a man who put aside a strong desire for peace and signed the nation's most important document, the Declaration of Independence. My duties also include the preservation of the site's historic structures, so that future generations can enjoy these traces of our historic past. I have sometimes found myself preserving these treasures in ways I had never imagined.

Although the official title is Thomas Stone National Historic Site, this place was known as "Haberdeventure" for most of the past 325 years. The first owner of the property, a man named John Barefoot, purchased 150 acres of land here in 1682 and named it Haberdeventure. He left no record of the meaning of the name or why he had chosen it. When Thomas Stone purchased the property almost 90 years later in 1770, he officially bought Haberdeventure and Hanson's Plains Enlarged properties. Stone dropped the last part of the name, but kept "Haberdeventure." For the next 200 years the name endured. In 1977, a fire destroyed the main section of the house and the name was dropped. After the National Park Service opened the property in 1997, the name was revived.

But what does the name Haberdeventure mean? A linguist on our staff came to the conclusion that Haberdeventure was taken from a Latin phrase that translates loosely as "A Dwelling Place in the Winds." That makes sense, because John Barefoot was a

198

Piscataway Indian, an Indian who was converted to Christianity and who was taught Latin by the Jesuits of the region. Visitors sometimes comment on the lyrical nature of the name and even wish that it was used in place of our more formal designation. The name does describe the site well. The property sits on a plateau. Just 500 yards down the road is the Port Tobacco River valley, a 50 to 60 foot elevation drop. As the highest ground in the region, the site experiences just what the original owner must have been thinking when he named it. It truly is "a dwelling place in the winds." During my five years here, I have experienced a fair share of nature's forces.

On April 28, 2002, a mere three and a half months after I started work, I learned what the winds of Haberdeventure could be like. When I left work that day the weather was partly cloudy and there was a possibility of evening storms. I arrived home an hour later and turned on my television. The news reported that Charles County, where Haberdeventure is located, was under a tornado warning. Thinking that there was no way that a tornado would actually hit, I turned off the TV and thought no more about it.

The next morning, I received a call from our maintenance foreman. I had been wrong. Less than two hours after I had left the site, an F4/F5 tornado, packing winds of up to 180 miles an hour, had swept through the park. The tornado stayed on the ground inside the park's boundaries for almost one full minute before continuing on its path of destruction through Charles, Calvert and St. Mary's Counties.

The good news was that Haberdeventure had not been damaged. The bad news was that we had lost our maintenance facility; its cinder block construction had not been able to withstand the tornado force winds. We had also lost an historic 19th century cattle barn. All of the park vehicles were destroyed except for one car that had been parked outside the area. Approximately 300 trees were felled, many of them more than 100 years old. The devastation was unbelievable. It seemed as though we had stepped onto a battlefield the day after the battle. I had never witnessed nature's fury on such a scale. Cinder blocks had been thrown through parked vehicles and insulation was driven through tree trunks like arrows fired from a bow. Yet even with all the damage we had sustained, we considered ourselves lucky. The tornado had struck after we had closed for the day and no one had been hurt. The work ahead was daunting. Cinder blocks spread out over a hundred yards, and there were downed power lines, broken glass and uprooted trees everywhere. The main park roads were blocked.

NATIONAL PARK SERVICE

Thomas Stone National Historic Site

There was an incredible amount of work to do before we could reopen the park. More than 50 NPS staff—including maintenance, law enforcement, natural and cultural resource specialists, and interpreters from parks around the region—pitched in to clean up the wreckage. We were finally able to reopen two and a half weeks after the tornado hit. Almost five years later there are still downed trees and other signs of damage throughout the park. They remind us of the tornado's devastating visit. This was not the kind of preservation that I had thought I would be doing when I accepted the job.

The winds of Haberdeventure returned with a vengeance the following year. Hurricane Isabel struck the mid-Atlantic states as a Category 1 hurricane, and the wind blew up to 74 miles per hour. Our sister park, George Washington Birthplace National Monument, received a direct hit; the monument lost numerous trees, suffered erosion of the beach area and the cliffs along the Potomac River, and had downed power lines that took more than two weeks to repair. Thomas Stone National Historic Site and Haberdeventure fared better. About 60 trees were lost in addition to the more than 300 downed in the prior year's tornado, but again we considered ourselves lucky. No one was injured, we did not have downed power lines, there was no major structural damage to any of the buildings and we were able to open again within a few days of the storm.

In November of 2006, two inches of rain fell in just over two hours, flooding the roads. In some places the water was almost two feet deep, and it created waterfalls in the park that had never been seen before. On the eve of the first two Christmas candlelight tours of the house in December 2002 and 2003, major snowstorms almost caused cancellation of the events. Along with times of extreme heat and humidity, snow, sleet, ice and pounding rain, Haberdeventure has definitely survived many of nature's forces.

For such a small park site, Thomas Stone National Historic Site has definitely had its share of excitement. John Barefoot probably knew exactly what he was doing when he named his property Haberdeventure. It is definitely the wind that causes the most concern. The staff knows to be watchful when Boreas, the North Wind, starts to howl. We listen to the shutters on the house rattle, we watch as the trees struggle to stay rooted and we pray each time that this storm is not the big one that might finally knock down the old house. Yet, like all of the keepers of this place over the past three centuries, we will stay and weather the storms. For Haberdeventure is now our "Dwelling Place in the Winds."

Packs Antelope

by Gerard Baker & Paige Baker

The first one of us to be attracted to the National Park Service was Gerard. Then within the last 5 years, Paige joined the NPS as well, due in part to our tribal beliefs and connection to the old stories of our people. Our tribal beliefs regarding our clan beginnings and about the forces of nature have always influenced us to respect the land. Our first creator said that you were not to destroy life. You could use what you had, but you were also supposed to save for future generations. See, that's hand-in-hand with the NPS mission. And it's a powerful tie.

We are members of two tribes, Mandan and Hidatsa, and it is from the Hidatsa side that we belong to the Low Cap (Apuka-weka) clan, which is matrilineal. This clan has the responsibility for the ceremonies that honor the Thunderbirds and ceremonies that are held to bring the rain, thunder and lightning and even the winter weather needed in the northern plains. We were raised to have great respect for our clan and for our father's clan, the Flint Knife clan. The Flint Knife clan have the responsibility of naming and burying our clan members; our mother's clan has many other responsibilities, including instructing the young about the many ceremonies and traditions that were passed down through the ages.

We still have a lot of the true traditional elders in our clan. When we were young we lived in a log house that our father built, and we had no electricity or running water; no television, radio or video games. Since we had no phones, people just dropped in. Visitors were always fed, no matter what time of day or night. After they had eaten, they always told stories of long ago. Our tribe lived in what we now call the five villages, which is now a National Park Service site called Knife River Indian Villages National Historic Site. Historically we lived as an extended family, not in nuclear families. Our people had earth lodges, not tipis. Growing up on our cattle ranch, we knew harsh weather, both extreme hot and cold. There were hard times, but we loved to listen to the elders and hear their stories in the Hidatsa language. We usually sat on the doorstep and listened carefully because the stories taught us the many different clan responsibilities. There were creation stories, stories about the earth and sky, and stories about what happened to our tribe and clan after the second smallpox epidemic in 1837. Our clan was forcibly relocated when the Garrison Dam was built—that really changed our lives and culture— our entire tribe was moved up from river bottom in the late 1940s and early 1950s. Many, including our parents, used wagons and a team of horses. Our father also had a Ford tractor that he used to pull a trailer house, while our brother herded the saddle horses. There's a book about that time, called *Dammed Indians* by Michael Lawson, that tells about the Pick-Sloan Plan and what it did to our people. You should read it.

Some of our sacred stories can only be told in certain times of year, but here are a couple that you might learn from.

Our explanation of a tornado has a direct correlation to our clan. You see, we believe the reason we have tornados is because of a fight between a large snake that lives in the Missouri River and the Thunderbirds. This giant snake, which, according to the elders, had his head at the confluence of the Yellowstone and Missouri Rivers and his tail at the confluence of the Mississippi and Missouri Rivers, was married to a lady called "The Old Lady Who Never Dies." When the Thunderbirds get into a fight with the snake, they pick up the snake from the river and they do battle over the prairie. This is the tornado.

We will now tell part of the story of the origin of our clan. In the spring, the young Thunderbirds molt to get their adult feathers so they can fly, just like all young birds still do today. When they molt in their nests, they shake and the winds take the molted feathers to a nearby lake we now call Demmick Lake. This action wakes up a large two-headed snake that is made from flint. The snake then slithers across the ground up the steep butte to the northeast and eats the young Thunderbirds. This was in a time before clans.

A young man who lived in the villages to the southeast (Knife River Villages) was named Packs Antelope and he was a great hunter. His medicine was the birds. He would

MARC MUENCH

Badlands National Park

pray to the four directions and the birds would come and tell him where the game was. He was an orphan, but he would always bring back the meat, which he would distribute to the elders and to those that did not have family members to hunt for them. While out on a hunt, Packs Antelope did not have any luck for four days. On the fourth day, he woke up before dawn and all around him was very heavy fog and a very bad smell. The elders said that it smelled like burning old moccasins. He realized that he was not in the same place where he had gone to sleep the night before, because the Thunderbirds had picked him up and taken him and placed him on a high hill with very steep sides. The sides were so steep that there was no way down. Remember, this was a time before the creation of clans. It was also a time when all beings depended on their various medicine powers to help them live.

He started to pray to the spirits that had helped him. He heard a female voice singing from a place he could not see because of the fog, so he went toward the singing and saw two small Thunderbirds. Then he saw a very heavy thunderhead cloud form with severe lightning and thunder and from that thunder he heard a voice that told him that grandfather had brought him to save the baby Thunderbirds which were being eaten. There was a fierce storm, with lightning, rain, hail and thunder. He was given four days to prepare to fight the snake with two heads. Packs Antelope then prayed to the four directions and to his medicine, the birds. From each direction the birds brought him advice and items he would need to kill the two-headed snake. For example, one direction brought him four arrows. From another direction, the birds told him how to kill the snake by opening its mouth and finding its heart.

The birds from another direction told him to take the four arrows and slide them on the ground. They told him that the two arrows that slide farthest were the two that he would use to open the mouth and the two that stayed with him were the two that would find the heart, for the kill.

The other birds from the other directions taught him the sacred songs he was to use for protection and also brought him two big rocks—one to the south, one to the north—to be used as shields.

Packs Antelope vanquished the snake as he'd been taught by his medicine helpers, the birds. Because of their help, he then prayed and invited all of the birds from the four directions to come and take this snake and feast. This is one reason that flint is found all

MARC MUENCH

Mount Rushmore National Memorial

up and down the Missouri River. Keep in mind that this was before birds ate reptiles, and from that day on, birds lived and still live on reptiles.

When Packs Antelope killed the snake, both of the heads slid down the hill, making two paths to be used to come down. Packs Antelope started to come down, but instantly a very big thunderstorm came upon him again, and again he got scared. A voice came from the Thundercloud telling him not to be afraid. It told him that because he had saved the Thunderbirds and mankind, as a gift they were going to make him half Thunderbird and half human. The Thunderbeing also told Packs Antelope that because he was half-Thunderbeing now, when he awoke, lightning would shoot from his eyes when he opened them in the morning. If he looked directly at anything, including his family, they would surely die. Packs Antelope was told that, in order to prevent causing harm, he should wear a head covering that would cover his eyes, so that when he woke in the morning, the lighting would hit the brim and be deflected to the ground. They also said that from now on, all of his descendents would be called "Low Cap" and they would be given the "right" to pray to the Thunderbirds to prevent bad storms or to ask for needed rain for the earth and gardens.

Packs Antelope became a Thunderbird and flew like the eagle. The old people saw him flying above in the sky and missed him and went to talk to The Old Woman Who Never Dies to help get him back. She went to her husband, who, as we mentioned earlier, was a giant snake that lived in the Missouri River and could do mysterious things, including putting his arms up near the surface of the water. This made it seem like there were lots of little snakes swimming around, which would attract the Thunderbirds and Packs Antelope. And it worked! Seeing the snakes, Packs Antelope swooped down to grab a meal and was dragged to the bottom of the river. There, a sweat lodge was built, and he was taken into this sweat lodge where he was beaten with willow branches. They switched him until he vomited up everything he'd eaten as a Thunderbird and became human again. He still had the power of the Thunderbird that emanated from his eyes and returned to the village to continue to help the elders.

Because lightning still came from his eyes, Packs Antelope realized that he couldn't continue to live with humans and went away. Every spring when the first thunder is heard, the elders remind us that Packs Antelope is coming back to help the clan, the village and the people. It is also the time that those that still carry this medicine bundle have to go back to the butte and feed the Thunderbeings so that they will continue to come back again to replenish earth and help grow crops. It reminds us of the power of the creator and that we all need to respect all living beings.

Our stories are a reflection of our people. Our respect for the national parks as the caretakers of our land is a part of our respect for the earth, the seasons, our clan and each other. Aho.

Science & Discovery

The Food Web

Life in the Most Extreme Place on Earth

In Search of Bear Scat

Discovering Cave Life

Protecting Pink Baby Spoonbills

Anyone who has ever visited a national park knows that they are special places, filled with opportunity for personal discovery. What you many not know, is that national parks are also a valuable source of cutting-edge research and scientific discoveries.

For years, national parks have served as outdoor classrooms, wonderful destinations for field trips. Busloads of students of all ages arrive daily by the thousands to learn about everything from how fire effects soil, to night sky programs on light pollution, to the endangered habitat of the desert tortoise. Students hear lectures, use scientific equipment, help with data gathering and become stewards of our parks.

New information is coming out of science projects in the parks at an amazing rate. The National Park Service and its partners work on hundreds of different projects throughout the system. At Great Smoky Mountains, as part of the all-taxa biological inventory project, scientists, teachers, students and volunteers have found over 4,600 species that no one previously knew existed in the park and have documented over 650 unknown species! Some of these discoveries could have wide ranging impacts. For example, some slime molds found contain cells that could eventually affect the treatment of Alzheimer's disease!

Studies done in national parks have contributed to our understanding of trends in global climate change. Detailed data has been gathered from computer modeling and satellite imagery of specific landscapes, especially glaciers. The weight of scientific evidence has allowed us to understand how greenhouse gases created by people are affecting the climate and the environment. Weather conditions and the effects on specific natural resources are also being studied and projected into the future. The application of what we learn today will have dramatic impact on the environment that we pass along to future generations.

Other fascinating research involves wild animals. For example, technology has helped provide a much better idea about grizzly and black bear populations in areas such as Glacier National Park. Bears rub against trees and leave bits of hair in the bark. The bears' DNA can be determined from hair samples through gene mapping techniques, which allows scientists to differentiate individual bears. Numbers, ranges and family groups can all be studied. The science that allows gene mapping was aided by discoveries made studying organisms that thrive in the hot springs at Yellowstone National Park!

In the Waterton/Glacier International Peace Park, radio collars equipped with global positioning systems are being used to track the seasonal migration and survival rates of bighorn sheep. Nearly 117,000 locations have been gathered so far from just 79 animals. Researchers also study sheep droppings for clues about how local bands of sheep interact over long periods of time. Preliminary data suggests some unexpected findings. By examining

DNA from samples, scientists found that groups of bighorns that are separated by less than 25 miles are as genetically distinct as humans of different races are from each other.

Great gray owls are being studied and much has been learned about their habitat needs and life cycles. Like many animals, these magnificent creatures have been impacted by human development. They suffer high mortality caused by automobiles. Owls fly low when chasing rodent prey, sometimes right across busy park roads. Scientists are searching for ways that humans can better coexist with all our friends in the animal kingdom, especially since our fates are so interrelated.

Many amphibians are disappearing from places where they once were abundant. For example, mountain yellow-legged frogs have disappeared from 95% of their historic habitat in Yosemite and the remaining populations continue to disappear at a rate of about 10% per year. Scientists are working hard to identify the causes of this decline. One cause that has been identified is the past introduction of non-native species for recreational fishing. Researchers have determined that fish predation resulted in a 50-80% decline in mountain yellow-legged frogs. While this may not seem important to your daily life, this rapidly disappearing species is just one indictor of the impact man has on the environment and the global food web.

In the early part of the 20th century, rangers removed every big predator that they could find, firmly believing that they were leaving the parks "safe" for deer, elk and other prey species. Back then, no one understood the fragile balance of nature—that prey species would actually suffer from overpopulation, starvation and disease when the predators were gone. Now we better appreciate the interrelation between different species and act accordingly. We protect all wildlife and vegetation in the parks. For example, wolves were reintroduced at Yellowstone, helping to restore the natural balance of that ecosystem. As John Muir said long ago, "Tug on anything at all and you'll find it connected to everything else in the universe."

Scientific discoveries happen every day in our national parks—challenging beliefs, informing decisions and changing the way we live. Some of these discoveries simply couldn't have happened anywhere else in the world. Imagine what you will discover on your next visit and what awaits scientists in our parks in the centuries to come!

The Food Web

by Cidney Webster

Ah, nature's food web. That filigree entanglement that links life and death, predator and prey—those that eat and those that are eaten.

Seeing the food web in action can be an awesome thing. In my career I've watched a black bear eat a mule deer, happily ripping out its entrails and gorging on the innards. I've seen a wasp drag a paralyzed tarantula back to its burrow for its offspring to feed on the spider's still-living body. I can safely say that at both those sights I was drop-jawed, mostly just to see live things that, up to then, I had only seen on the Discovery Channel.

Gob-smacked though they were, I don't think that the six-year-olds on my education program felt that same sense of wonder and respect for nature that I did on their first live viewing of the food web in action.

In 2000, I was the education coordinator at Fort Point National Historic Site, which is located in the Presidio of San Francisco. I ran a program for five and six year-olds called "Sensible Habitats." The point of this program was to introduce kids to the notion of habitats and the different creatures that live in them.

It's a cute program for kids that age. First they meet and observe a terrestrial critter, 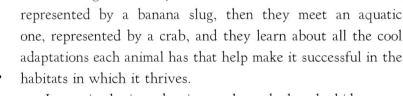 represented by a banana slug, then they meet an aquatic one, represented by a crab, and they learn about all the cool adaptations each animal has that help make it successful in the habitats in which it thrives.

It was in the introduction to the crab that the kids got an extra lesson.

In that portion of the program the kids are led out onto a

ED KASHI

Golden Gate National Recreation Area

concrete pier jutting into the bay. For safety reasons I have the kids all sit down well away from the pier's edge.

As the kids watched, my intern, Mike, and I pulled out of the bay a crabbing net we had cast before the start of the program, and plopped it on the pier hoping to see one or more crabs clinging to it.

That day we caught one crab and used it to talk about adaptations needed to survive in an ocean environment—we talked about the way a crab walks, with this crab being particularly cooperative and providing a demonstration. We talked about how and what it eats. We determined whether it was a boy crab or a girl crab. The kids looked at its eyes, counted its legs, avoided its claws—in short, Mike and I built a strong relationship between the kids and the crab.

After all this, Mike held the crab aloft and I asked the kids, "Should we keep him or should we send him home?"

"Send him home! Send him home!" All the kids shouted back.

"Okay. On the count of three we're going to throw him back into the bay. Ready? One. Two. Three!"

What I noticed, but hadn't paid much attention to, was a gull standing to the side of the kids on a concrete wall, watching our whole display with the greatest attention.

What was this bird up to? Was it hoping to get tossed a few crumbs, or maybe that the kids might leave behind some tasty treats?

Oh no! It seems that he had something much better in mind because the second our beloved crab hit the water, the gull swooped down off his perch, scooped up the crab, landed on a near-by ledge and proceeded to rip it apart and eat it in front of the children.

Just then came one of those moments—a moment when a second takes a long time to pass, and time seems to have stopped until something jars it back into motion.

In that very long second, Mike and I looked from the gull to the children and saw twenty pairs of round eyes and mouths in perfect little circles. There was no sound but the wind and waves. Mike and I looked from the kids to each other and tried not to laugh, and some snarky parent standing behind them said, "Well, that's the food chain!"

The second caught up with itself when the kids, en masse, jumped up from where they were sitting and lunged toward the edge of the pier to see if it really was their crab the gull was eating. Mike and I snapped to and barred their way before they could all knock each other into the bay. After all, safety is our top priority. We hustled the kids off the pier, trying to divert their attention from the gull dining unashamedly on our favorite crab. They certainly would have much to discuss on the bus ride back to school about natural habitats and their newfound exposure to the stark realities of the food web.

After we waved good-bye to the kids and their bus pulled away, Mike and I went back to the pier to collect our crabbing equipment. Passing the concrete wall I saw that the gull was gone and all that was left of our crab was a claw and a bit of shell.

Those kids are now all young men and women, and I wonder what, if any at all, influence that experience had on them. I wonder how those kids remember the experience, if they remember it at all. For me it was a slightly awkward interpretive moment and an ironic surprise, something Mike and I laughed about for a long time afterward. Maybe that incident served as an introduction to nature's sense of humor, and hopefully, now that the kids are older, they can appreciate the joke.

Ah, nature's food web—that delicate dance for survival, those ties that bind us to being nourished or being nourishment. There's nothing like seeing it in action!

Life in the Most Extreme Place on Earth

by John Varley

I always suspected that scientists seemed to enjoy baffling their audiences with obtuse language, Latin phrases and mind-numbing equations, but I never understood why. Why would they work against their own self-interest? I knew that each one of them had really swell science stories to tell, at least when I talked to them in private, but in front of an audience it was as if a thick jargon-gene automatically kicked in.

Uninvited, I tried to compensate for them. I attempted to make their stories simple and comprehensible so that I would have great science stories to tell. After a while it became like a game for me. Could I really explain something that was very complex and technical in plain and simple language? My proof for a successful story was simple—visitor understanding. The language I used I called "layman-ese" and the story structure was what a TV journalist would call "sound bites."

My game became a lot harder in the early 1990s when Yellowstone was first flooded with a new type of researcher that used a whole new language. It was then that the tools of science were being revolutionized by PCR, short for the polymerase chain reaction. Now, there is a phrase to write home about! It's a great example that supports my point. This chemical reaction gave scientists the ability to take DNA from any living specimen,

plant or animal, and clone (duplicate) a tiny quantity overnight into an amount of DNA large enough to be thoroughly studied. By itself this was a remarkable achievement, but for biological scientists it was earth-shaking. For the first time they had the ability to explore the huge new world of genetics with a level of precision and depth that scientists of a half-generation before could only dream about. It was also entirely different from my

MICHAEL FREEMAN

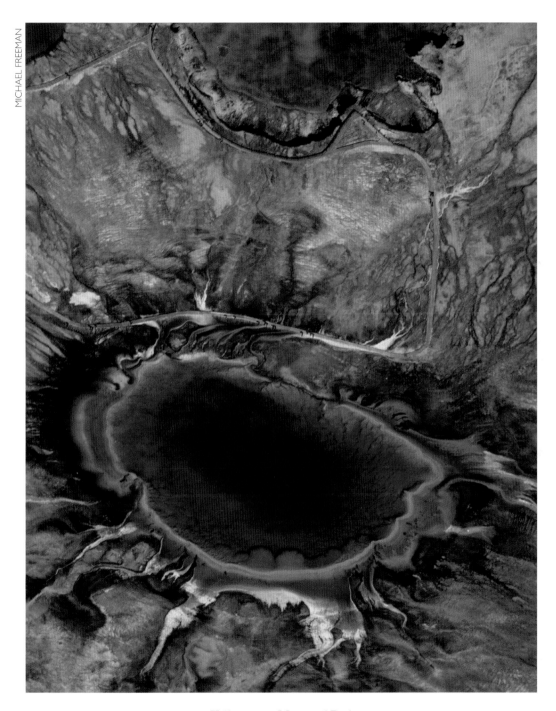

Yellowstone National Park

aged world of genetics, when we speculated about the genes for male pattern baldness and genetic improvements were considered done when a superior male of any species was bred to a superior female. Times have changed!

As a process, the PCR had been kicking around laboratories for while, but it didn't become a big success until an enzyme was discovered that allowed the chemical reaction to perform at high temperatures. That's when PCR became revolutionary. Most astonishing for me was that the enzyme that made it all possible was discovered in a Yellowstone hot spring organism. The enzyme became known the world over as Taq polymerase.

But why should you care? Let me count the ways. Perhaps you should care because the polymerase chain reaction starring Taq polymerase is now playing in a laboratory near you. In case you missed it, it may have been playing under its common alias: DNA fingerprinting. So if a criminal leaves behind one strand of hair or one drop of blood, and if the police capture it, it can be cloned by PCR into billions of exact copies overnight. The genetics from just one cell can be turned into perhaps a thimbleful. This, in turn, allows typing (precise characterization) of the genetics of the perpetrator and vastly increases the odds that the criminal will be caught. To me, that's remarkable, but PCR magic works in the reverse too. We've seen many news reports about people leaving prison because the convicted person's DNA did not match the DNA left behind at the crime scene, captured by police or stored unanalyzed in an evidence room. So PCR often works for exoneration as well as convictions. Bless Taq polymerase!

Catching criminals is old news for people who use PCR and Taq on a daily basis. Many diseases are now diagnosed using this reaction. The overnight test for HIV/ AIDS is an example of one of its common uses. Take either criminology or medicine, and DNA fingerprinting is now a big part of our brave new world. There are many other applications in the fields of biology, genetics, agriculture and pharmaceuticals, all prime users too, but you should be getting the revolutionary picture by now.

Taq was discovered from a Yellowstone bacteria species named Thermus aquaticus, one of a large group of microbes collectively known as extremophiles because they live in environments that are so severe, or extreme, that the majority of life on earth would perish if placed into that environment. Thermophiles (heat-loving) are one division of these extreme organisms. Thermus aquaticus enzymes don't break down when heated in the PCR process. The fellow who had the ingenuity to discover Taq and make it an indispensable part of PCR won a Nobel Prize for his creative efforts. In a take-off on Time magazine's "Man of the Year," the journal *Science* named Taq the "Molecule of the Year" for 1995, in what may have been the first time any chemical molecule was so honored. The industries created by PCR and Taq have generated billions of dollars. In the world of science and business, Taq and PCR were huge hits.

Now, this is all great stuff, and really good Taq stories could be told for virtually any of the aspects mentioned above, but there is a lesser told story about the bizarre world of extremophiles and thermophiles that interests me the most. One that few people know about.

Yellowstone National Park has over 10,000 distinct geothermal features. They come in the form of geysers, springs, mudpots and fumaroles. While they're all hot, the temperatures have a huge range—from about 60°F to over 220°F. They also have an extraordinary range in pH, from ultra acid (near zero on the scale) to high alkaline (pH 11.3). Each thermal feature has its own rich geochemistry as a result of differences between hot water interactions with soluble minerals deep in the earth. The result of all of these variables is that at the earth's surface, we have an almost infinite number of habitats available for thermophiles to grow. Scientists studying these organisms have identified and named over 500 thermophilic species thus far. Some scientists believe that the biodiversity is greater in the park's hot springs than in equatorial rain forests, but that remains to be seen.

When we compare our normal world with the thermophile world, there are few similarities. I'll try to make this story as simple as possible. In our world plants eat photons from the sun and make them into useful compounds for animals to consume. We humans then can eat the plants directly or the animals who eat the plants. In contrast, many of Yellowstone's thermophiles have adapted to eat very different things, such as sulfur, iron or arsenic, and they're not dependent on the sun at all! One of my favorites has no common name and is called only by its Latin name, Sulfalobus. As the name suggests, it has a very strict diet of sulfur, and sulfur is most common in highly acid hot springs. So it turns out that Sulfalobus only thrives in boiling sulfuric acid. You and I might only live a second or two in this environment, but Sulfalobus not only thrives in it, it requires it. It might be tempting to conclude that they have found their own Nirvana, but alas, it's not true. It turns out that, just like humans, they suffer from parasites and viral diseases too. They live among other species that have adapted to boiling sulfuric acid, so they too have competitors for food and space. We can conclude then that Sulfalobus lives in a complex interactive ecosystem, just like we do, but unlike ours, it's an ecosystem that is rare on earth and very extreme.

The next time you go to Yellowstone hoping to see giant grizzly bears or wolves, be sure to also look for some of the park's smaller and more extreme inhabitants. Most of the wonderful colors in the park's many hot springs are not minerals, as many people believe, but rather colonies of microbes. I hope you enjoy and appreciate this scene, because Yellowstone is one of the very few places on earth where you can see microbes in nature with the naked eye. It's one of even fewer places on earth that you can see microbes that are extremophilic and thermophilic. Perhaps the next place you see these words, it will be in a news reports about the discovery of life in outer space. After all, something that can thrive in boiling sulfuric acid could have just what it takes to survive on other planets. So in the future, when you hear about extremophiles, you can just sit back and tell all your friends in layman-ese, "It's no big deal, I've already seen them in Yellowstone!"

In Search of Bear Scat

by Todd Nelson

It was my sixth and final season as the Manning Camp ranger in Saguaro National Park. Working ten days straight, then taking four days off, I always started back to work about 4:30 a.m., hiking up out of the Saguaros to the vanilla-scented ponderosa pine forest. I left early, at least an hour before the sun came over the ridge, because the moment the sun rose, the temperature would begin to climb. The lows during the summer nights usually hovered around the high 70s to low 80s, but at dawn the temperature immediately felt 10-15 degrees warmer.

My commute involved a four-hour trek through six life zones of the Sonoran Desert, 9.3 miles of hiking, up 4,500 feet in elevation to the pine forest at 8,000 feet. Part of the trail was like walking up never-ending flights of stairs; in fact, there are actual steps cut into parts of the trail. At the end of the climb was Manning cabin, my home for yet another ten days in the cool mountain air. At the end of ten days, I would again hike down for four days off. This was a five-month-long ritual that I enjoyed for six summers.

As the Manning ranger I had many duties: I managed the comings and goings of staff, worked as a wildland firefighter, purified water for drinking, responded to medical needs and repaired trails. One of my favorite duties involved working with researchers.

A study conducted by investigators at Saguaro National Park and the University of Arizona involved collecting bear droppings ("scat"). The object of the study was to find out how many black bears were living in the Rincon Mountains in the park. The project was part of a larger study, which sought to document bear migration patterns in southeast Arizona. My job was to collect scat samples, photograph them and record their size. The investigator planned to collect bear tissue cells from the scat. The cells from each sample would be tested for DNA. The DNA evidence from the scat samples could be linked to individual bears, which in turn would provide an estimate of the number of bears in the Rincon Mountains.

One day, I decided to search for scat on the North Slope Trail. It is on a remote section of the mountain, where I had always come across a lot of bear scat in the past.

In June of 2003 a fire in the area had burned really hot in some sections, leaving a moonscape after it passed. Two years after the fire, portions of the trail were badly eroded and it was hard to find any sign of it. Even though I was familiar with the trail after hiking it at least a dozen times, I found that it was easy to get off trail for a short period. I decided to start at the west end because that is where it is the trickiest.

Since I would be working alone, I did a few things to help ensure my safety before I left the cabin. I secured a can of bear spray on my pack within easy reach. I put my battery-powered park radio on my waist clip for easy reach and tossed a set of fresh backup batteries into my pack. I made sure that I had plenty to drink and eat. Most importantly, I marked my planned route on the Plexiglas-covered topographic park map on the wall.

It was a beautiful day for hiking; the blue sky was dotted with a few puffy clouds, the wind was blowing through the trees (my favorite sound), and, best of all, I was being paid to hike! (OK, I was being paid to hike and pick up bear poop, still, not bad!) Less than a mile up the North Slope Trail and... success! I could almost see the steam rise off a black/brown mass filled with acorn shells! Fresh! There were no tracks on the trail, so I couldn't tell what direction the bear was traveling, but I knew that it had been right in this spot only a short time ago. I turned on the GPS unit to record the location and then got out the rest of my equipment—rulers, markers, camera, notebook and a baggie (you can guess what goes in there). On the baggie I noted all the pertinent information, including the mass, width, length and height. I took a picture and, using the baggie as a glove, retrieved the sample. I then sealed the bag and tossed it into my pack.

After about an hour, I came to a section of the trail that was hard to follow. I debated which way to go. After a few minutes of searching, I picked a route near a rock outcropping and again began to look for scat. I quickly found another fresh pile. I put my pack down and started the collection ritual again, but then I saw another and another and another—a

TOM GAMACHE

Saguaro National Park

total of nine! Nine fresh piles of poop! I was definitely earning my pay today!

With all that fresh scat, I started to worry about what might be waiting for me just down the trail on the other side of the rocks ahead. I radioed the visitor center to let them know where I was and what I was doing. I promised to contact them again in 30 minutes to let them know I was okay.

What was going on? How could nine separate deposits have been made at nearly the same time? Bears don't hang out in groups! Soon after mating, the male and female go their separate ways and the female raises the young on her own. Cubs travel with their mother for 18 months and a sow usually has two cubs. Two of the scat samples appeared to be from adults, others from juveniles and others from cubs. I knew that this was virtually impossible, as sows only breed every other year. Even so, I started to imagine all nine bears in one spot and got really nervous. My imagination worked overtime with possible scenarios, none of which involved me ending up as a healthy, old ranger.

Over the next two hours I radioed the visitor center every 30 minutes to let them know that I was still alive and working. As I was collecting the data for each specimen, I looked up nervously and often to see if I could spot bears. Each time I heard the slightest noise, I nearly hurt myself trying to see where the sound came from.

Having already collected the nine samples, I decided to hike all the way around the rock outcropping. I radioed the visitor center with GPS coordinates—just in case. I had made very little noise during the collection process, hoping that it was true that bears hear only moderately well. Their sense of smell is really good, though, so I should have noticed which way the wind was blowing, but I didn't. My mind was elsewhere! Each time I came around parts of the rock outcropping, I wondered, with my heart in my throat, what was going to be there. I was almost back to my pack—having walked all the way around the rocks—and had found no more scat and no bears at all. I kept imagining what it was like just a few hours before I arrived.

Heading uphill toward the trail, I found yet another pile, but it was not as fresh. As I lifted the sample I could see that maggots had moved in; hard on the outside, but gooey on the inside, good for them I guess. I radioed the visitor center to let them know that I was leaving the area and that I would contact them again later. I came to another section of the trail with a rock outcropping next to it. The last one was so productive that I decided to search near this one too. I found three more samples; all had been there a long time and were hard and light. Into my pack they went.

I never did come upon a gathering of bears—what an experience that could have been! But the truth is that I was relieved. Even though it's well known that black bears rarely hurt people, I was not prepared to be the only human in a group of nine bears. The memories of that day will stay with me for a very long time.

Discovering Cave Life

by Gretchen Baker

We held on tight as we jolted along the overgrown two-track road, trying not to bump our heads on the ceiling of the old Suburban or fall all over each other. Although it was warm out, we had the windows rolled up to avoid having tree branches whip our faces. To call this a road is generous, but the five of us were happy to absorb the shocks along the way—we were in search of new cave life.

I am an ecologist at Great Basin National Park, where we are working on a biological inventory of several caves. Three cave biologists were with me that day, along with Meg, another park staff member. The cave biologists had traveled a long way for this bouncy ride: Steve came from the Illinois Natural History Survey, Jean from Zara Environmental in Texas, and Mike from the The Nature Conservancy in Arkansas. All have had years of experience, especially when it comes to things that live underground. They had made many new discoveries and had helped to protect caves so that the delicate creatures that live in them can survive far into the future.

When the road ended we got out with our gear in large backpacks. We stretched our legs on a 45-minute hike to the cave, bushwhacking through thick vegetation and gulping for extra oxygen because of the high elevation. We climbed higher and higher, skirting rock outcroppings, avoiding a patch of rose bushes. Finally, we came upon some old metal water troughs.

The water troughs were a welcome sign, since we were headed to Water Trough Cave, which had been named for the nearby landmark. We climbed up another hill and found the cave entrance arching over our heads. Tangled vegetation blocked our view into the back of the cave, and we pushed through it to

TOM GAMACHE

Great Basin National Park

arrive at the edge of a pool that extended about 30 feet to the back of what looked like a small room. A long time ago someone built a dam at the cave entrance. It trapped water that was sent through a pipe to the water troughs below, but even on that wet spring day, there wasn't enough water to spill out of the cave.

In addition to the water in the pool, the cave entrance room is notable for the large brown stains that cascade down the side and back walls. These stains are underneath pack rat middens. A midden is a pile of trash near a pack rat nest. The pack rats collect objects like twigs, seeds and animal bones and pile them on top of each other. In order to make the mound stick together, they urinate on it. The middens have a distinct odor that is dank and sweet at the same time. As I looked into the pool that filled most of the entrance room, I saw that material from the middens was visible just below the surface. I also suspected that the water hid not just mud, but also pack rat guano (droppings).

While the cave biologists and Meg started inventorying the cave entrance area, I volunteered to take a first look deeper inside the cave. I'd been caving for over ten years and always enjoyed being the first one in. Plus, my curiosity had the better of me and I was anxious to find out what was hiding in that back passageway. Having been forewarned that this cave was quite muddy, I slid some fishing waders over my jeans and secured them with suspenders. I put my notebook, vials and tweezers in my small front pocket, and fixed my helmet and headlamp securely on my head. I was ready to enter the dark abyss.

Great Basin National Park has over 40 caves within its boundaries and each cave is unique. Some are wet and some are dry. Some are at lower elevations and some are so high that they can only be entered in the summer when the snow melts away from their ice-coated entrances. Some are beautiful, like Lehman Caves, where public tours are offered, while others are barren of formations. Some have streams running through them and flood periodically, while others are dry and dusty. Very few are large enough to allow walking upright for long; most require crawling and even belly wiggling. Fortunately Water Trough Cave has an entrance that is large enough to allow an upright entrance.

I stepped gingerly into the pool and immediately sank in over my boot. The mud and guano mixture was obviously deeper than it looked. I moved cautiously to the opening at the back of the entrance, and found that the mud was getting deeper. As my foot sank in, a foul odor was released—a mixture of sulfur and pack rat urine. Obviously some decomposition was occurring around my feet. I turned on my headlamp and took a step into the dark. The passageway was tall but narrow, and the mud was up to my knees. I kept one hand on the wall for balance, pulled up a foot and heard the slurping sound of the mud releasing my foot. I stepped forward, wondering if there was a floor below the mud or if there would be a sudden dropoff sending me pitching face forward into the gooey concoction around my legs. I found firm footing, but it was deeper than I expected. With my next step I sank farther. The cold murky mixture was pressed against my legs. I wondered if this was what it felt like to be in really smelly quicksand. Uncertain about how deep I might plunge, I continued on slowly, my eyes adjusting to the dark and the small beam of light from my headlamp.

The passage widened and I had to decide which way to go. Would the left or right side be safer? I stayed to the right, hoping that I had chosen wisely. The next couple of steps took me farther down into the mud, but then I found some footing that was higher. Inch by inch, I began to emerge from the ooze, which coated my waders in black slime. With a deep breath I reassured myself that I was not going to disappear into the murk and begin looking closer at the cave walls. I found some small flies clinging to the surface and made notes about them.

The passage made a turn and became narrower, but I was able to get partly out of the mud. Just beyond a small calcite bridge I found a piece of wood with a dead rodent on it. I wondered if it hadn't been able to find the way out. Knowing that most of the cave ecosystem is based on guano and dead things, I examined the rodent carefully, rolling it over with my tweezers. Success! I saw tiny creatures moving under the carcass. Small worm-like creatures wiggled about. Then I saw two minuscule white critters moving. I was very excited, since often all-white creatures in caves are endemic, found only underground. They do not have any pigment because they don't need any. These creatures had probably never seen the light of day—or any light, for that matter. I bent closer, and using a magnifying glass, took a closer look at one. I saw that it had many legs, possibly a hundred, with two legs attached to each segment. This fascinating creature was a white millipede. I put it into my vial, being sure to take note of the location. As I continued forward, the cave passage got smaller, and eventually I was crawling through the mud. I came to a wall of white cave draperies, a formation that totally blocks the passage and stands in stark contrast to the muddy floor. At the bottom of the draperies there was a small trickle of clear water. Only diminutive cave creatures could go farther, so I turned around headed out, looking for more invertebrates along the way. I found some beetles and flies and another white critter, a springtail—so named because it moves by using its tail to spring ahead. Since I knew that I wouldn't sink into a bottomless chasm of sucking mud, I walked quickly and was out of the cave in less than ten minutes. I excitedly told the cave biologists about my finds. I gave them my waders and they disappeared into the cave.

It took awhile to clean up from the trip, but we eventually got the stink of the mud and guano off and bounced back down the road. The cave biologists made some preliminary identifications of the specimens we had collected, then sent them off to specialists. After a couple of months, we heard some exciting news. The white millipede that was in such stark contrast to the dark mud turned out to be a new species, called Idagona lehmanensis. It had never been seen anywhere else on earth—and I helped make this discovery! All of a sudden, our trip into the dark, gooey, smelly cave seemed really important, which was something I wasn't thinking about after taking that first step into the thigh-high black slime.

Protecting Pink Baby Spoonbills

by Cara Cooper

"Don't move!" Jerry called softly. We had just discovered a spoonbill chick still in its nest. Jerry threaded his way through the jumbled mass of mangrove roots to get to the nest quickly. We knew that spooked chicks are likely to leap out of the nest in fear, which is frequently lethal. Jerry, weathered and rugged from a decade of doing wildlife surveys in Everglades National Park, was surprisingly nimble as he picked his way through the bizarrely tangled vegetation, whereas I had already tripped twice.

From an eye-level nest in the mangrove tree in front of me, a tiny bird's black eyes peeked out as it cowered and cried in fear with a faint, constant squeak. In spite of what initially looked like a bear-like grip, Jerry gently scooped up the chick before it had a chance to test is featherless wings and spoke soothingly to calm it down. It seemed to settle a bit as Jerry warmed it with his hands.

Even though the chick was covered in white fuzzy down, long winter cold spells can be deadly if spoonbill parents leave the nest for too long. This baby spoonbill seemed to be a late bloomer, as the rest of the colony had already fledged. Jerry smiled like a little kid as he inspected the tiny bird and leaned closer to sniff the chick. I laughed, thinking that it can't be a very pleasant smell, since spoonbill chicks are fed

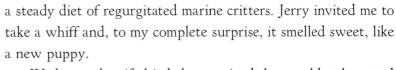

a steady diet of regurgitated marine critters. Jerry invited me to take a whiff and, to my complete surprise, it smelled sweet, like a new puppy.

We knew that if this baby survived, he would only spend a few more weeks in the nest before his parents began to teach him to fly. They do this by landing a short distance from the nest when they return with food and then coax the chick out of the nest to get its dinner. Each time they land a little farther away, forcing the baby to hop from branch to branch, and eventually the chick follows them in flight to get its tasty meal. It is really quite ingenious and I wished that my dog were that easy to train. Once the chick has learned to fly, it begins following its parents to the feeding grounds. Spoonbill chicks learn to forage for food by the time they're seven or eight weeks old.

Unfortunately, there are many obstacles in a baby spoonbill's path. In 2005, Jerry and his team of researchers at Audubon's Tavernier Science Center became alarmed when they noticed a massive nesting failure at Frank Key, the third largest spoonbill colony in Florida Bay. In 2003, spoonbills at Frank Key successfully reared 64 chicks; in 2005, just six chicks.

Jerry described the many potential causes of death for spoonbill chicks, including falls from nests, predation, sudden low temperatures, starvation and parasites. However, the drastic decline at Frank Key was a mystery to the researchers, since none of the usual signs of a massive nesting failure were present.

To investigate, they began making observations from the water to see if something peculiar about Frank Key was causing the problem. Spoonbills naturally avoid nesting on islands with raccoons, which ruled out roughly two-thirds of Florida Bay as nesting habitat. Had one of those sneaky critters made it out to the island? No, that didn't seem to be the problem. Instead, what they noticed was increased boat traffic around the island. The grass flat near Frank Key was once an area that fisherman silently poled around but in the last few years that has started to change. As boats increasingly buzzed the island or fished the shoreline, the adult spoonbills had become more easily spooked, leaving their nests vulnerable. Opportunistic feeders such as crows and black-crowned night herons are incredibly smart and have started to take advantage of the situation. To them, the sound of a motorboat approaching is, as Jerry says, "a dinner bell." After witnessing an attack by a horde of crows and night herons, Jerry was stunned. Their response to the sound of the motorboat was so quick that they were on the exposed nests almost as soon as the spoonbill parents had been spooked away. It took less than a minute for the crows to inflict lethal damage.

While Jerry finished relating the heartbreaking story of Frank Key, he completed his inspection of the chick and put it back into the nest so we could move on. We trudged through the strange, dense interior of the island to find the larger colony of

ARTHUR MORRIS

Everglades National Park

fledged birds on the opposite shore. The island reminded me of the bizarre planet that Yoda called home in Star Wars.

By then I was thinking that the problem could be solved if the spoonbills would just start over when a nest fails. Jerry explained that they usually couldn't. He described how spoonbills primarily nest in Florida Bay from November through March. A very specific set of conditions was required to initiate nesting, which must continue in a very specific sequence. If at any point a link in the chain of events is broken, they give up and usually don't try again. In the past, ill-timed releases of water due to water management practices have flooded spoonbill feeding grounds. This caused spoonbills to abandon their nests, since they weren't able to find enough food for their chicks. In October 2005, Hurricane Wilma barreled through the park, leaving the majority of trees on spoonbill nesting islands leafless and bare. This compounded the predation problem, because, without the camouflage of leaves, the spoonbills and their nests were easily spotted. When exposed, spoonbills are even more likely to take flight when they see a potential predator approaching.

To help prevent further disturbance to the nesting populations at Frank Key and Sandy Key, park rangers temporarily closed the moat around Frank Key to boat traffic, as well as the campsite at Carl Ross Key. Sandy Key was permanently closed to boat traffic a few decades ago since it is a major rookery for many wading birds, bald eagles and osprey, in addition to the spoonbills. In general, with the exception of North Nest Key and Little Rabbit Key, which are designated as campsites, all other islands in the park are closed to landings. Boaters should stay more than 300 feet away from rookery islands between November and March. This helps to prevent disturbances to nesting birds. If you find yourself accidentally flushing birds from their perches, you are too close—please back away and allow the birds space to usher in the next generation of our feathered friends.

Jerry and I eventually emerged onto the far shore of the island and the sight took my breath away. There were hundreds of deep pink adult spoonbills and light pink juveniles. This was the main colony where the majority of the recently fledged spoonbills would spend time following their parents around, slowly building their strength and testing their wings. We quietly waded into the water and stood perfectly still to survey the birds. I recorded the tag numbers that Jerry quietly whispered to me.

I could hear the soft whooshing sound of wings all around me. I slowly looked up and saw dozens of the agile parents and their wobbly young. They were flying just a few feet overhead, oblivious to our presence. From this vantage point, I could see exactly why the spoonbill has become a symbol for the beauty of Florida Bay—a wonder to be enjoyed and preserved by all of us—locals and visitors alike.

Life Changing Experiences

A Cinderella Story
~ GREAT SMOKY MOUNTAINS NATIONAL PARK ~

18th Street School ~ South Central L.A.
~ SANTA MONICA MOUNTAINS NATIONAL RECREATION AREA ~

The Last Walk
~ CARLSBAD CAVERNS NATIONAL PARK ~

History Through the Eyes of a Child
~ FORT CAROLINE NATIONAL MEMORIAL ~

The Day America Was Attacked
~ NATIONAL CAPITAL REGION ~

The Keeper of the Flame
~ STATUE OF LIBERTY NATIONAL MONUMENT ~

Every park ranger has heard, "Oh, ranger, what do you love most about your job?" The question is both easy and difficult to answer. It's easy because the answers are almost always inspiring, but it's difficult because there are so many answers.

"Oh, ranger, thank you so much for saving our boy's life!" Each time a ranger hears praise like that, it's a life changing experience for everyone. The family's life is forever changed by the ranger and the ranger's life is forever changed by the family. It's safe to say that every park ranger knows stories about inspiration and change. The most important is usually about his or her career choice—that life-altering decision to put public service and conservation above other factors, including pay. (Ranger's often joke that they are paid in sunsets!) Another story that every ranger knows is the one about Stephen T. Mather, a central figure in the creation of the National Park Service. Mather was a very successful businessman and could have continued on that path, but when he started visiting western parks he was disgusted by what he saw. He wrote a pointed letter to Secretary of Interior Franklin K. Lane, detailing the deplorable conditions and mismanagement that he had witnessed. Instead of a polite response explaining the government's position, Mather received a letter that changed his life. Secretary Lane threw out a challenge: "If you don't like the way the parks are being run, why don't you come to Washington, DC and run them yourself?!" That's just what Mather did, becoming the first National Park Service director in 1916. (At that time there was no central authority to manage national parks, even though land had been federally set aside for public enjoyment as early as 1832, when the Hot Springs Reservation was created in Arkansas.) Instead of going on to amass a greater fortune in private business, Mather's commitment to the national parks was so strong that he even spent his own money when federal appropriations were inadequate to take care of the parks. Just imagine if we had that kind of commitment from government officials today!

Life changing experiences can occur at almost any time in a ranger's life. For example, one day a ranger decided not to issue a young couple a ticket when he saw that their dogs were off leash. Instead he spent time talking to them about wildlife preservation and need to preserve other visitors' enjoyment of the park. A 20-year friendship was born. The couple spent many of those years as volunteers at Santa Monica Mountains National Recreation Area. Another example is when a ranger's childhood friend, who had been paralyzed since her late teens, learned that she was offered a position as a ranger. (She ultimately became a superintendent in a national military park!) Such stories change the lives of all those they touch and are in inspiration to countless others.

Successful search and rescues missions are always inspirational, but the most powerful life altering experiences inevitably involve children. Ranger programs, "Parks-as-Classrooms" presentations and even chance encounters can all spark a child's lifetime commitment. Sometimes a ranger gets the feedback immediately, but the truly lucky ones get feedback years later, when the then-grown child shares the events that changed their lives with "their ranger." Especially in these cases, the ranger comes away with renewed energy and commitment.

In the late 1970s, three college students from eastern cities named Barbra, Rob and Bob signed up as volunteer Student Conservation Association aids at Canyonlands National Park. Their season in remote districts of the park were spent patrolling the backcountry, staffing the ranger station, and giving guided hikes and campfire programs. They were so inspired by their experiences that Barbra went on to work for the US Forest Service, Rob became one of the leading authorities on American Indian law for the US Solicitor's Office and Bob joined the National Park Service, ultimately becoming the superintendent of a national lakeshore. SCA-sponsored interns have been working alongside rangers in the parks for years and many of them have returned to work in all facets of park management. Other interns are recruited specifically because they might have never otherwise visited a national park. Outreach programs—some sponsored by cooperating associations and others by major corporations—allow culturally diverse students to spend their summer vacations learning about our natural and cultural resources, serving visitors, assisting scientists, helping with resource management projects and much more. All leave these experiences forever changed for the better.

National parks are among the most beautiful and inspiring places in the world. They provide all who enter—whether rangers, park workers or visitors—with magical moments they'll never forget. The sight of a bald eagle soaring, a mother grizzly ambling across a meadow with her cubs, a sunrise reflecting off a spectacular peak or simply a moment's interaction with another person—all these moments find places in the heart to live and grow. All these moments continue to change our lives forever.

A Cinderella Story

by Toni Huskey

Have you ever seen the movie "The Other Sister?" This movie is a portrait of my family. I was born with cerebral palsy in Tennessee during the 50s. Seeking more knowledge on how to raise a child with this disability, my parents moved to Michigan. They soon discovered opportunities to receive financial aid. We benefited from the encouragement of other families with disabled children. In Detroit, I attended a school for children with disabilities. I received speech and physical therapy classes. I have one sister, Brenda, two years younger. She was the normal one. I had a dream that someday I too could live a normal and productive life without being so dependent on others. My parents made sure I received proper treatment but many assumed I would never be able to live a normal life.

My father worked in an automobile factory and my mother was a school crossing guard. We did okay. I spent summers in the rugged mountains of East Tennessee with my grandparents, who taught me the family history and how difficult it was just finding a place to settle and call home. My grandmother, Hannah, told stories about the old times when our family barely survived from season-to-season. She was a woman with many talents, making almost anything from nearly nothing, especially using and re-using flour sacks. She made dresses, aprons and underwear from flour sacks. She even made mattresses for her children by sewing several sacks together and filling them with corn shucks.

Grandmother had a cellar where she made moonshine. Many people came to visit her. Everyone left that underground room happy, including grandmother! She believed it was important to taste her creations before she sold them. One night all three of us

MARC MUENCH

Great Smoky Mountains National Park

girls who stayed there that summer—my sister, my cousin and me—were sound asleep when grandmother came in yelling, "Get up!" She took us to barn and, you'll just never believe this, she said that something had landed in the loft and that little men came out! Well, we know now that grandmother was having a bit of a moonshine hallucination trip. She did more than just make moonshine for income. She took me to clean rooms with her at the Gatlinburg Inn (it's historic and still there) and taught me how to make things gleam.

My most memorable Christmas was spent with my grandparents. It snowed on Christmas Eve and, using their imaginations, my grandparents took two planks, dragged them through the snow and across the porch, added some cow droppings, and left Santa's huge bag of toys on the porch. Gazing out the window, seeing this overwhelming evidence, all of the children instantly became true believers in Santa and his reindeer.

I got married right out of high school, moved back to Tennessee and had two beautiful children, a boy and a girl. I was very sick when I was pregnant with my son, so sick that I got dehydrated and weighed only 87 pounds. When he was born, my son had severe cerebral palsy. He can't walk or talk. I kept him with me until he was about five, but then I had to admit that I needed full-time help. He lives near me in a nursing home, where I visit him every day. My husband had left us after only two years. We got married really young and he just couldn't take it, I guess. My parents moved back to Tennessee to help me, because I just couldn't do it all on my own. I went on welfare and was on it for quite a few years. My daughter is normal and healthy and she's been married 17 years. She lives in Sevierville and has a son. I talk to her every day.

I discovered that life sometimes takes unexpected turns and embarked on a new journey. As a single mother, with two precious children to raise, I found an opportunity to work for the National Park Service at Great Smoky Mountains National Park. I was employed for a decade as a seasonal maintenance worker. Excited to have such a wonderful opportunity, I envisioned having that job for the rest of my life. Looking back, I admit that there were occasions where I would look starry-eyed at the uniform catalog, wondering what it must be like to wear a ranger uniform, with the golden NPS badge and that familiar flat hat. I knew in my heart that I would never be able to wear such a uniform, because I had a limited education and my only experience was cleaning (though I was an expert "commode-ologist."). No matter, I was thrilled to have an opportunity to work in the park and took great pride in every aspect of my cleaning job.

Sometimes, when I'm asked to tell a "clean" story from my maintenance days, I like to tell about a very important meeting in the training room. My supervisor instructed me to make sure that everything was exactly right. Well, the coffee pots were filthy, so I came in extra early that morning, filled them with bleach and left them to soak. I went to finish a job in another part of the building, intending to return shortly to rinse out the pots and make fresh coffee. Well, someone beat me to it and made the coffee using the water in the pots! Now these were very important people in this meeting, even some from TV. They took their coffee outside and, well, you can imagine what happened next. I tell you, they were spitting coffee everywhere! Some happened to be standing next to cars parked outside and that coffee took the paint right off. I thought for sure they'd fire me on the spot—oh, the job insecurity—but it wasn't really my fault and so it all worked out okay. It's definitely one of my better "clean" stories!

One summer day, the park's new chief of interpretation stopped by to introduce himself. Chris must have seen something in me that no one else had ever noticed. Perhaps he noticed my enthusiastic interactions with visitors or somehow got a sense of my knowledge, love and passion for people and the park. Chris gave me a gift for which no amount of thanks will ever be sufficient. He arranged a transfer for me to become a National Park Service interpreter—a ranger! So there I was, with little education, a major disability and work experience that was limited to performing routine maintenance tasks. How could I do it? How could I go from cleaning toilets to donning a green and grey ranger uniform? It was overwhelming, but I thought that if he could take such a leap of faith with me, then there was no way I could possibly let him down. I had to prove to the world that I could be a wonderful interpretive ranger.

My newfound job offered me many unexpected benefits. Suddenly, I found myself in a position to inspire and encourage others with disabilities, especially children. Who was better equipped than I to present interpretive programs to these children? I was able to enroll in educational courses and learn new computer skills. I took advantage of every opportunity. I even traveled to the Albright Training Center at the Grand Canyon—named after the first superintendent at Yellowstone—and was fortunate to be able to visit several different national parks along the way. I've researched and created computer-generated slide presentations, which I've presented to many groups. I have led walks and talks in the most beautiful place on earth, helping visitors to find their "inner hearts," transporting them to a different place and time.

I'm especially thrilled when I get to present Junior Ranger Certificates. I hope it's not bragging to say that kids are drawn to me and love my special techniques. I love educating them about stewardship and the principles of "Leave No Trace." I demonstrate how much fun it is to discover life in one of the few places on earth that remains largely untouched by man—a place that development will never be allowed to destroy. I teach them about the habitats that only exist in the Great Smoky Mountains. Lots of children come through our park thinking it's just a playground. After I spend time with them— explaining the exhibits and talking about why we have national parks—they leave with a different impression. Children are quickly drawn to want to learn more about their surroundings and how to care for our parks. Many parents have taken photographs of me with their junior rangers. I hope that the experience is something they'll look back on fondly as they grow up. I, too, cherish each of these encounters, all part of my amazing national park journey.

I love my ranger uniform! I was even selected to model it for the national park uniform catalogue. I still can't believe it was actually me on those pages! What an honor to represent this amazing profession. Once I was selected as "Employee of the Year!" I felt like Cinderella. Because my roots are here in Tennessee, I feel a special connection with this park. I feel that it's my responsibility, actually my privilege, to educate visitors about the sacrifices that were made to create what is now the Great Smoky Mountains National Park. I can show them why this place is unique and should be special to everyone. Sometimes, I use a prop or two, maybe a flour sack, so that I can talk about my grandmother Hannah and her life in these mountains. Out on the trails I talk about the animals that can only survive in this unique ecosystem. We have salamanders that just can't live anywhere else. We reintroduced the elk, river otter, peregrine falcon and native trout. They'd all either suffered from loss of habitat or had almost been hunted to extinction.

My work is my life support. All my feelings of fulfillment come from my work and from the people I interact with every day. I have overcome huge obstacles in my life, bettering myself with each mountain I climbed. Visitors, staff and volunteers help me overcome the emptiness that I sometimes still feel inside. Now don't you think I'm having a pity party! I live in a beautiful home that I bought all by myself. I have a new car and the security of health and life insurance. Every day, I glow with inner happiness, so thankful for having been given a chance to succeed. Visitors who meet me see nothing but joy and always leave with more than they had when they arrived. Before I close my eyes at night, I make sure that both of my children know that I love them and thank God above for helping me along on this marvelous journey. My life is so full, all because one man saw something special in me and believed in me in ways that even I couldn't imagine. So now I do my best to thank him every day by working hard to educate and inspire those I meet, with the hope that maybe I'll be able to use this great gift to make a difference in someone else's life.

18th Street School
- South Central L.A. -

by James Laray

> *The early Greek philosophers looked at the world about them and decided that there were four elements: fire, air, water and earth. But as they grew a little wiser, they perceived that there must be something else. These tangible elements did not comprise a principle; they merely revealed that somewhere else, if they could not find it, there was a soul of things—a Fifth Essence, pure, eternal, and inclusive."*

Freeman Tilden

Spring of 1992 marked a terrible time in the history of Los Angeles and the whole United States. Violent images of the Rodney King beating dominated news broadcasts across the country and excerpts of the controversial trial polarized America. When the judge announced the verdict of "not guilty" that April in Simi Valley, the city fell apart. Riots wreaked havoc throughout Los Angeles, primarily in South Central, and the eyes of the nation and the world were riveted on news reports that portrayed the chaos—smashing, burning and pillaging. Anger and distrust ruled.

Stationed at Santa Monica Mountains National Recreation Area, just 30 minutes north of the city, my duties as a park ranger extended downtown during this time of

need. As a recent hire, labeled as the "new guy," my assignment took me to the education centers of the Los Angeles Unified School System, where I was to spread the message of the National Park Service. At first, the idea of being stuck in commuter traffic didn't thrill me—my passion was to work at the Native American Cultural Resources Center or conduct nature hikes, but I had a duty to fulfill.

Santa Monica Mountains National Recreation Area

Before the race riots in Los Angeles, my boss had urged me to implement "ranger in the classroom" programs at schools in South Central LA. The sentiment was that if they couldn't come to the park, we'd take the park to them. Initially, I didn't wholeheartedly embrace the idea, but the events of that spring reinforced the primary reason that I became a ranger. I believed that the National Park Service was an example of American goodness and the ranger, with flat hat and gold plated bison badge, was the one who carried the message. It bothered me that our message was not reaching all Americans. Although downtown L.A. was a dangerous place, wrecked by riots and filled with thugs who hated outsiders—especially outsiders in uniform—I decided I would face the fears and fulfill this urban mission. All of my colleagues believed me to be insane.

One early morning in May, I revved up the white ranger cruiser and headed for my metropolitan destination. My heart pounded as I watched the affluence and glamour of the San Fernando Valley melt away in my rear view mirror. I slowly entered a world of barbed wire, gang graffiti, burnt-out storefronts and desperate mothers peering from behind steel-barred residential windows. I was filled with fear of the unknown.

I chose Watts because of the 67 riots in its history and, of course, due to the most recent riots. To me, it was "the heart of darkness," the place I feared most and also the place I felt most needed.

I followed the street signs to the elementary school—a school with only a numbered location for a name—18th Street School. The schools in the comfortable suburban neighborhoods where I had grown up had warm gentle names like Plum Tree and Willow Lane. I didn't know what to expect at a school with such an uninviting name. As I meandered down a side street, I noticed bullet-riddled buildings and cars. I slowly drove up alongside a group of African-American teenagers hanging out, leaning against a car. They looked menacing and bored, and by my estimation, should have been in school. Adrenalin shot through my chest and my palms began to sweat as they glared at me with hardened expressions. Would they approach my slow moving vehicle, or worse? I felt so out of place—a sitting duck driving a car with the arrowhead logo plastered on the door, and a big green stripe running down the side stenciled with "PARK RANGER." Almost in dream-like fashion as I rolled alongside these young gawking men, I distinctly saw one mouth the words "park ranger?" To this day I remember his expression of disbelief and amazement as if to say, "What is a park ranger doing in 'the hood'?" He seemed completely disarmed, curious and intrigued, and, as a result, no longer a threat in my mind. I almost felt giddy, as if I had exceeded his ability to imagine a uniformed officer coming in peace.

I found the public elementary school and was directed to park inside a gated compound to avoid having my vehicle stripped or stolen. The building was in perpetual lock down. As I approached the front, a couple of plainclothes LAPD detectives saw me, with my signature flat hat adjusted two fingers above the bridge of my nose.

"What the heck are YOU doing here?!" one blurted out in stunned amazement.

"I'm here to educate the students about the wonders of our national parks," I explained to the surprised men. "Why are you here?"

"To pick up a 6th grader and take him down to the DA's office on an arrest warrant," one responded. They bid me a sarcastic and foreboding "good luck" as I entered the building.

At the epicenter of arguably the worst riots experienced in the USA—in a school filled with children without role models, from broken homes and poor families—I found out just what it means to be a park ranger. I found my purpose. Teaching those children about the messages that guide me changed my life, not only in my career as a park ranger, but as a person. I will forever remember their bright eyes and unyielding eagerness to learn. It was magical.

The kids loved me! I had been to many schools in my career, including many in affluent areas, but never before had students and teachers received me with such excitement and gratitude. In society's eyes, these kids had nothing, yet they still were pure of heart, unbroken by the harsh reality of their environment. It was as if I were Santa Claus. I felt that I was doing exactly the right thing! Never before did I have the opportunity to make such a positive impact on the lives of others. In the words of Freeman Tilden, the father of park ranger interpretation: "I was touching the ephemeral fifth essence."

Back when I was at Ocmulgee National Monument, the Indian mounds in Georgia, my first chief ranger thrust a worn copy of Tilden's seminal work, "Interpreting Our Heritage" into my hands. I received this book even before being issued my uniform. He simply said, "Read it, memorize it, live it!" When people asked me what language I was interpreting, I explained myself in the philosophy I learned from Tilden. I was interpreting the park for them—its hidden beauties, perhaps even its soul. I invited them to join me in its love and protection.

In South Central, I ventured out for lunch with one of the teachers. Along the way I received a quick lesson in gang spray painting and learned how to determine "Blood" and "Crip" territory. At the restaurant, I was mobbed by everyday citizens who were amazed to see a real life park ranger. It was as if I were a movie star. I wondered if some of my impromptu admirers were gang members, as some sure looked the part. At that moment, however, they were simply teenagers in search of something to fill a void, one I was happy to satisfy. Beneath their tough facades, their eyes revealed childlike wonder. I received question after question about lions, tigers and bears, all the while thinking to myself, "Oh my!"

I spent the next week with that school in that neighborhood. Later I visited the wondrous Watts Towers—a national historic landmark administered by the National Center for Cultural Resources. I met many wonderful people there and many strong friendships blossomed. We invited a large group to come up to the wilds of the Santa Monica Mountains National Recreation Area and they accepted. You couldn't miss them during our multicultural festival—a sea of young and old wearing stunning African kente cloth clothing. I discovered that these inner city kids, fueled by misconceptions and too much TV, were threatened by the unknown of the pastoral setting, just as I had been intimidated by my unfamiliarity with the inner city. That day we all found peace and grew together despite our different ways of life. The pain I'd felt from watching the horrible race riots of 1992 was healed, and I could see my guests' faith in humanity was on the mend as well. In my 15 years with the National Park Service, I cannot think of a more significant experience than my week in South Central Los Angeles.

It was a true victory.

The Last Walk

by Constantine J. Dillon

Anyone who has ever had a job knows that it's not uncommon for work to sometimes seem routine. National Park Service rangers are no exception. While our jobs are often set in spectacular environments, we sometimes take for granted the amazing beauty, history and culture that surround us every day. If we're not careful, we can also easily forget that our actions can have great impact on the people who surround us. Fortunately, I learned this lesson early in my career.

Years ago, I was one of the many rangers who patrolled the trails of Carlsbad Caverns National Park. Every day, for eight hours a day, we walked the cave's one-way loop trail in the opposite direction of pedestrian traffic. Visitors, attentively listening to audio tours, often missed out on some of the wonderful details of the cave. It was in a similar fashion that they sometimes ignored live rangers. At times like this, many rangers thought themselves superfluous, their jobs boring and meaningless. Yet all people seem to want to connect with others and the appreciation of a new place is certainly enhanced through interaction. The experience of exploring the cave can definitely be made much richer by talking to a knowledgeable ranger. It was up to us to entice the visitors away from the recorded voice and back into the real world.

So, whenever it struck our fancy, we would approach visitors at random, using our flashlights to highlight unseen features, while interpreting the hidden secrets of the cave's natural environment. To be honest, it wasn't uncommon for the male rangers to choose to strike up conversations with pretty girls and for the female rangers to be more inclined to stop and talk to handsome young men. One day, I randomly stopped to talk to a family that consisted of an older gentleman, a young couple and their children, all of whom were patiently walking the trail and listening to the recorded tour.

"Would you like to see something neat?" I asked. When they responded positively I proceeded to give them a lesson on the geology of the cave, pointing out a variety of formations along the trail and explaining how they came about. Everyone was attentive and appreciative. When I finished, they thanked me and continued their walk along the loop. An hour or so later I came upon the same group again. This wasn't unusual because rangers walked along the one-way trail a bit more quickly than the visitors—and in the opposite direction. They recognized me immediately and asked if there was anything I could show them in this section of the cave.

Excited to be doing real interpretation, I eagerly pointed out more formations, talked about the cave's history, answered their questions and generally had a good time making their visit—and my day—a little more interesting. Again, they thanked me and continued on. Having met hundreds of visitors on those busy summer days, I went on about my business, continuing on my patrol route and thinking nothing more about this encounter. Yet, this one turned out to be something more...

About an hour later, I was heading to the elevator that would take me to the surface. The elevator is located near the cave's underground lunchroom, where the family was having lunch. They spotted me, called me over, greeted me with enthusiasm and told me what a great time they'd had. After a little more discussion about the cave and how wonderful their visit had been, the older man paused and looked at me. "You know," he said, "we live in El Paso and I have been through this cave many times over the years, but I have never seen it like I did today." (That certainly made me smile!) "You showed me things I never noticed before and made this the best trip I've ever had here." If he had stopped right there, I would have left on a high that would have carried me for a week. But instead, he added something else that I will carry with me for the rest of my life. "What made this visit particularly meaningful," he said, "is that because of a medical condition, this is the last time I will ever be able to walk through this cave, or anywhere else. You see, next week I have to have both of my legs amputated." I was glad that the cave was dark because the tears welling up in my eyes and the knot in my stomach made it impossible to talk to any more visitors that afternoon.

MARK TOMALTY

Carlsbad Caverns National Park

I will never know what made me choose that particular family to talk to on that particular day, but the experience has been a guiding force throughout my career. As a park ranger, I know that I have the potential to help create lasting memories for each and every visitor I meet. That day at Carlsbad Caverns taught me that I'd never know when a visitor might help do the same thing for me.

History Through the Eyes of a Child

by Daniel R. Tardona

Young Bethany stared at me intently as I told the Fort Caroline National Memorial story to her 4th grade class. Little did I imagine that the experience she had that day would have a long-lasting effect on how I viewed my job as ranger. Nor did I know that it would change my perspective on the story of Fort Caroline. I was still fairly new to the site, but I had conducted this same interpretive program at least a hundred times for school groups.

Part of my job is to try to help visitors find meaning in historic events of the past. Most people can relate to things that pique their curiosity or that touch them in some way. It's fun—but also a challenge—to provide that experience to members of a large group of young children on a warm, sunny northeast Florida day.

Fortunately, all the emotional and curiosity-inspiring elements that can catch kids' attention are inherent in the Fort Caroline story. During the 16th century, France was competing with Spain, the world's leading power, to stake a permanent claim in La Florida. This was about 60 years prior to the historic Plymouth Rock landing far to the north. French settlers struggled for survival in the new world and braved all kinds of danger in the hope of acquiring wealth, having adventures and gaining religious freedom.

Helping the French to build the fort and village were some very different-looking people, the native Timucua Indians. Two of the students enjoyed acting with wonder and suspicion, mimicking what the French and the Indians may have felt as they met for the first time. All eyes were glued on me as I told them that the settlement barely survived its first year. They looked perplexed as I told them that despite initial good relations with the Indians, the colonists began meddling in Indian social and political affairs and soured the relationship. Little clenched teeth appeared between their lips as I said that French interference eventually led to conflict between the colonists and Indians and that by the following spring the colonists were close to starvation.

There were surprised looks and a few giggles when I mentioned that Caroline was not a woman. The name is derived from the French *La Caroline* after King Charles IX of France. The children seemed riveted as they heard about how the settlers lived in constant fear of attack by the Spanish. The French Protestants, or Huguenots, were considered a religious threat to the Catholic Spanish. There were a few sighs when I told the children that a year after the fort was built, the Spanish did attack, and many of the men, women and children of the French colony were massacred. They gazed at the fort gate, presumably imagining the events of the past, as I began to close the program with my usual dazzling ending. It included the fact that those battles between the French and Spanish were the first that European nations fought for control of land in what is now the United States.

I prepared to close by leaving the group with one final thought, but was interrupted by an impressive barrage of questions from the slightly upset and extremely reflective Bethany. "Why didn't the French know how to get their own food? Why didn't they let the Indians tell them how? Why did the Spanish not like the French, or the Timucua Indians? How come the French, Spanish and Indians couldn't talk to each other and try to grow food together and learn about each other's religious stuff without fighting? You said that there were no houses or roads, but lots of woods, animals, oysters and other stuff to build houses! Couldn't all these people find different places along the river to live and share their stuff? You said that the French came because they were curious, wanted to find a better place to live than where they came from! You said the Indians wanted to learn about some of the new things the French brought with them even if they were a little scared. You said the Spanish wanted to make the Indians learn about their religion—maybe the Indians' religion was just fine!"

When she was finished there was an astonished silence. I am certain that my face looked much like those of the teachers, a few parents and the other children—eyes open wide and mouths agape! All the questioning faces looked trustingly at me for a response. It was a rare opportunity to amaze the audience with a brilliant response—or time for a

NATIONAL PARK SERVICE

Fort Caroline National Memorial

panic attack! With my mind racing and hands twitching I realized for the first time that my fascinating story about Fort Caroline was a story about failure, about how the human race failed to learn from its history of intolerance, greed and prejudice. I could feel the despair in Bethany's words. How was I to turn this story into a positive and meaningful experience for these children? In the past, I'd ended hundreds of similar programs with the question, "Who do you think won, the French, Spanish or Timucua Indians?" Then I'd take a vote and lead the group to the brilliant conclusion that nobody really wins in such conflicts. I also emphasized that the Timucua Indians lost the most, as their culture no longer exists. In hindsight, and after meeting Bethany, that seemed a very ho-hum conclusion!

At that moment I lost all confidence. My mind raced, but I could not think of a fitting response for this group of 4th graders. To buy some time, I said, "Those were all very good questions, Bethany, and we should all think about them." Then I asked, "Who do you think won, the Spanish, French or Timucuans?" I was still frantic because I knew that I had to get back to Bethany's questions. While I waited for responses from the group, I was saved. Young Bethany herself provided the insightful response!

In answer to my question, Bethany offered the best response of the morning, or maybe ever. She said, "If all those people would have figured out how to get along with each other, they might have started America sooner." I was stunned all over again, but this time I recovered quickly and asked her to explain a little more about what she meant. Bethany went on, "Well, we all don't believe in the same stuff here. We all live in Jacksonville and get our food from the same stores and don't fight—well, most of the time." She looked at her teacher and asked, "Isn't that what America is supposed to be about; people from different races and religions living together to be free?" Rescued, I was able to offer Bethany's response back to the group.

A lively discussion followed about the fact that what had happened at Fort Caroline more than four hundred years ago was still important today. Some of the children chimed in and related the story to what was playing out in other parts of the world in places like Bosnia and in the Middle East. They expressed their ideas about the United States: that though it is not perfect, Americans try to solve the problems of intolerance, prejudice, injustice and even the preservation of natural resources! They agreed that perhaps the human race did learn something from the mistakes made at Fort Caroline. The children concluded that the idea of the United States at least offered hope.

I saw the significance of the Fort Caroline story a bit more clearly that day and experienced a completely different perspective on a story that I've told hundreds of times. I learned that visitors, no matter their age, could provide perspective and insight into the meaning and relevance of our national park sites. My interpretive programs at Fort Caroline were forever changed because of the insight I gained from seeing the story through a child's eyes. Young Bethany reinforced that there is hope for the future, as long as we continue to learn from the past.

The Day America Was Attacked

by Einar Olsen

Tuesday, September 11, 2001, started out as a perfect autumn day. The sky was clear, the temperature was in the 70s, there was no wind and the humidity was finally low after many months of oppressive summer weather in Washington, D.C. I was the regional chief ranger for the National Capital Region of the National Park Service at the time, and was enjoying the beautiful day.

I was leaving my office on Hains Point just south of the Jefferson Memorial when a colleague told me that a plane had crashed into the World Trade Center in New York City. I didn't think too much about it at the time, because as a native New Yorker I knew that anything could happen there. When I arrived at the Anacostia Naval Station for a meeting, I learned that a second plane had struck. I knew immediately that it was a terrorist attack. Everyone at the meeting was distracted and our minds were not on the business at hand. Shortly after the meeting started, cell phones and pagers started to go off. A Defense Department agent took a call and announced, "The Pentagon has been hit!" We all raced to a big bay window and saw a huge plume of smoke in the distant sky. Everyone hurried out, each knowing that there were going to be much more important things to do that day.

Returning to the regional office, I met with the regional director and his staff. Everyone was visibly shaken. We could see the fire and smoke from the Pentagon just across the Potomac River. We quickly advised all parks in the D.C. area to close. Then I checked in with the U.S. Park Police headquarters next door to determine what help they needed. The park police provide law enforcement services in some of the urban national parks. They asked me to

PAT & CHUCK BLACKLEY

National Capital Region

call out 15 of the region's 45 law enforcement rangers. Shortly thereafter the regional director dismissed all remaining employees from our office. I was the last person in the building. After many attempts to contact the regional communications center by land line and cell phone, I gave up. I knew that the phone system had been overwhelmed. Everyone in the D.C. area was trying to reach their loved ones. I took one of the service vehicles and established radio contact with the communications center. I directed the 15 rangers to report to George Washington Memorial Parkway headquarters, about eight miles north of the Pentagon, where a staging area was being set up. After fighting my way through heavy traffic, I found Dana, a ranger with a great deal of experience with wildfires and other disasters, already at work. Together, we coordinated ranger response to three areas: Camp David (the presidential retreat), the Pentagon and the National Mall (the open area between the Lincoln Memorial and the U.S. Capitol).

TWENTY-ONE DAYS AT CAMP DAVID

The president's retreat at Camp David is in Catoctin Mountain Park in northern Maryland. The park is under exclusive NPS jurisdiction, and our most important function is to provide a secure buffer around the compound. That morning, Roger, the long-time chief ranger there, had received an urgent request from the Secret Service to close the park, as "protectees" would be arriving shortly. A veteran of innumerable presidential visits and other special events, including the Camp David Peace Accords, he immediately put the park's closure plan into place. At this same time, he heard an erroneous media report that Flight 93 had crashed at Camp David. He knew of the attacks in New York but had not yet heard about the Pentagon.

Soon the motorcades of protectees started to roll into Camp David, which would serve as an important nerve center for weeks to come in developing America's response to the attacks. Officials included Vice President Cheney, National Security Advisor Rice, Secretary of Defense Rumsfeld and Secretary of State Powell. The park was closed for the next 21 days and intermittently for an additional 24 days thereafter. Rangers from around the region and the eastern United States worked closely with the Secret Service, military, and state and local police to meet special security needs. I recall rangers and Secret Service officers detaining a couple who were touring America. They were on their way to visit the site of the Camp David Peace Accords signing. They claimed to be unaware that the U.S. had been attacked. The extraordinary circumstances of that morning forced us to become suspect of anyone who presented even slightly unusual behavior, especially in the area around Camp David. They turned out to be typical tourists but, as a result of the attacks, our view of the world was forever changed. America had entered a new era and, in our role as protection officers, nothing would ever be typical again.

THE PENTAGON DAYCARE KIDS

Dwight, the Chesapeake and Ohio Canal National Historical Park district ranger, was getting his law enforcement vehicle serviced that morning. While waiting, he saw a television report about the attack on the Pentagon. He left immediately to meet with his ranger staff. He made sure everyone filled their coolers with bottled water, knowing the type of assignments that awaited them in the capital. When the regional communications center instructed them to respond immediately to a staging area, they were already packed and ready to go. The sense of urgency and anxiety was extremely high. Traveling at speeds close to 100 mph, they reached the site in 45 minutes. (Dwight would later go on to become a driving instructor at the Federal Law Enforcement Training Center in Georgia.) The calm and confident Dwight was put in charge of the first squad to go out. Many of the group didn't know their way around D.C. very well, so I led Dwight and six other rangers in a convoy to the Columbia Island area of the George Washington Memorial Parkway, where our role would be to aid and protect the children and staff that had fled the Pentagon daycare center. I left Dwight to take charge and immediately returned to the staging area to get the next squad ready.

Dwight later described the whole scene near the Pentagon as surreal. He and other rangers were incredulous. They could not believe what had happened or what they now needed to do—take care of children from the Pentagon daycare center! Everything had happened so fast: first the news of the attacks, then the order to respond to D.C. as fast as possible, then racing to meet the children and staff.

Dwight took charge of the 50 children and their caregivers and worked to find a better location for them. It was with good foresight that Dwight had filled the coolers earlier. Dwight ordered an empty tour bus to be commandeered to transport the children. Led by a ranger vehicle escort, everyone was taken to a Virginia Department of

Transportation maintenance site about a mile from the Pentagon. During the drive, the rangers and the children could clearly see the damage to the Pentagon and the fire and heavy smoke still billowing from the building. Many of the day care personnel gasped when they saw the impact site. Until then they hadn't understood what had happened, because the daycare center was on the opposite side of the huge building. The children didn't seem to understand exactly what was going on, but surely picked up on the extreme tension and stress felt in the adults around them. Throughout the whole ordeal, the squad did everything possible to maintain a calm and professional demeanor, while focusing their attention on the needs of the children.

Once at the maintenance facility, the rangers set to work establishing a secure perimeter at the site. The children slept and played games. It seemed important to keep them occupied. Arrangements were made to get diapers and pizzas delivered. As parents arrived to pick up their children, rangers carefully screened everyone for security purposes. Two children who were usually picked up by their mother were instead picked up by the father. Sadly, their mother had been killed at the Pentagon that day. When all children had been picked up, the rangers provided the daycare staff with rides to their vehicles or homes. By evening, I released all the rangers to return home, as the shocking events of the day quickly began shaping our new reality. Starting the following morning, Dwight and the others would begin serving special security details at Camp David.

QUIET ON THE NATIONAL MALL

Back at the staging area, I put together another squad of six rangers. I led this squad southbound on the George Washington Memorial Parkway into Washington, past the Department of the Interior and on to the National Mall. By this time, much of the downtown had been emptied and the area was eerily quiet. I hope that Washington will never be that quiet again. There were no people or cars in the streets, or planes overhead. The city was deserted. Rangers worked with the park police to set up security perimeters around the National Mall and the Jefferson Memorial. Our squads remained on duty there until after 10 p.m., when they were relieved by park police officers.

NATIONAL PARK RANGERS IN THE 21ST CENTURY

Since 9/11, the job of national park rangers has changed. Like all of our fellow citizens, we have adjusted to the many new challenges that came after that day, serving in our newly defined roles with pride. Rangers in the National Capital Region and other areas of the country have been heavily involved in homeland security. They have assisted in special events assignments such as the 2002 Winter Olympics in Salt Lake City—providing perimeter security at backcountry ski venues—and during the official July 4th celebration in Washington, D.C. by screening visitors and providing other security functions. Rangers have also assisted at large demonstrations, donning riot gear along with their urban colleagues in the park police. After 9/11, many rangers were recruited to serve as air marshals, as part of the effort to get planes and travelers safely back into the sky. While the rangers' roles as protection officers remain relatively unknown, we remain dedicated to keeping our national parks—and all of America—safe and secure.

The Keeper of the Flame

by Charlie DeLeo

I've always loved the Statue of Liberty. It's been a special place for me ever since I first visited her as a nine year old schoolboy with my fourth-grade class. That was back in 1957. Years later, when I returned as a Marine from Vietnam in 1968, I just had to see Lady Liberty right away. In my Marine uniform, I took the Circle Line ferry to Liberty Island. I was the first visitor to run up to the statue's crown that day. Peering out her windows, I could see the upraised right arm holding the torch aloft. I had always wanted to climb to the torch, but I knew it had been closed for years—since 1916, in fact. Later that morning, I stood in front of the statue and looking up at her I said, "Dear God, before I die, can you just get me up to the torch one time?"

In early March of 1972, out of work, I decided to visit Lady Liberty to collect my thoughts in her crown. Halfway over on the ferryboat, a thought came to me: why not ask for a job there? Upon landing on Liberty Island, I went straight to the administration building and asked for a job application. I filled it out there, turned it in and went home.

A week later, I got a phone call asking me to come down for an interview. The chief of maintenance and the chief ranger interviewed me. To my joy and surprise, I was hired as a temporary maintenance worker for six months.

Right from the start, I longed to climb to the torch—and after a couple of weeks, I did. Early one Monday morning, a few hours before the statue was opened for visitors, I unlocked a metal gate just below her crown. This led to a 42-foot iron ladder that reached up into the torch. At the top of the ladder, I unlocked a metal door that opened onto the circular catwalk outside. The view was truly beautiful. The scene was fantastic. The New York harbor and the

VINCENT DIPIETRO, NATIONAL PARK SERVICE

Statue of Liberty National Monument

Manhattan skyline were spread out in front of me—bridges and buildings, including the twin towers of the World Trade Center, which were still under construction. In a strong wind, the torch and right arm would sway as much as six inches each way.

The "flame" was made up of 200 pieces of yellow-tinted glass enclosed in a shell of copper bands. There were ten large 1,000-watt light bulbs mounted inside the torch, which gave the flame its light. This stained glass arrangement was installed in 1916, replacing the original 1886 flame, which was made of solid copper sheeting.

I couldn't believe how dirty it was on the inside of the flame. There was dust everywhere. I started to clean the inside of the glass flame and replace the burnt-out light bulbs, all on my own time. For weeks, I came to work early every day and climbed to the torch to continue cleaning.

One day, my boss called me into the superintendent's office. I thought I was going to get fired for climbing into the torch, because I knew it was off-limits to everyone. The superintendent was an army veteran of World War II. He looked me over and then said, "Charlie, I've understand that you go up into the torch regularly."

"Yes, sir, I do," I said.

"Is it true, what I hear? That you're cleaning it and changing burnt-out light bulbs on your own time?" he asked.

"Yes, I am," I answered again, just waiting to be shown the door.

What he said next changed my life forever. "Charlie, we can't seem to get anyone who wants to go up there to take care of the torch. Do you want the job?"

I was shocked and said, "Yes, sir, I'd pay for the honor."

That's how I became the "Keeper of the Flame" of the Statue of Liberty. I went up to the torch the next morning and thanked God for sparing my life in Vietnam and for answering my prayers. A week later, the superintendent gave me a promotion. I was to be a full-time employee of the National Park Service!

I worked at the Statue of Liberty for more than 27 years before I retired in the fall of 1999. I made more than 2,500 climbs to the torch during those years. I inspected the lights about 100 times a year. I also took care of 70,000 cubic feet of the statue's interior superstructure. I had to wear a safety belt and a backpack vacuum cleaner while I climbed around the girders. I'd vacuum all the dusty sections of the statue's interior skin, wash down and paint her iron girders, and change burnt-out light bulbs.

As the statue's 100th birthday approached, the National Park Service set about restoring her. They realized that the 1916 stained glass version of the flame had been leaking water, which was corroding the torch. So in 1986, they replaced the glass flame and most of the damaged torch with a replica that reproduced the design of the original 1886 flame and added gold leaf on top of its solid copper sheeting. Sixteen 250-watt flood lamps were mounted outside on the copper walls of the circular torch catwalk. They were automatic and would light up as soon as it got dark, thanks to an electric eye. They reflected off the 24-carat gold flame—making Liberty's new flame many times brighter than the old glass one that was illuminated from inside. The original torch, with its 1916 flame, was placed in the lobby of the statue's pedestal, for all the visitors to see. I became the first "Keeper" to ever care for two torches and flames at the same time.

Sometimes I even had to climb atop the new golden flame to wash off the bird droppings. What a view from there! I must thank the National Park Service for the many times it has allowed newspapers, magazines and television crews to do stories on my work as the "Keeper of the Flame." There is one really special story I'd like to share. About ten years ago one of my coworkers, a ranger named Gene, asked me if I would take him and his girlfriend Lesia up to the torch. I said okay and arranged with Gene that I'd say I had to check on something down below in the statue, so he could close the torch door and have some time alone with Lesia on the catwalk. I climbed halfway down the torch ladder and waited. About eight minutes later, the door to the torch opened and Gene called me back up with the words, "She said yes!" I had known that he was planning to propose and it was great to be in on the secret. His future wife immediately realized this when she saw my face and said, "Oh, so you were in on this together?!" We all laughed. That was one of the happiest moments I've ever had at the statue and I know that Gene and Lesia will always treasure their time alone up on Lady Liberty's torch.

After I retired from the National Park Service in September 1999, I came back to the statue as a volunteer. Recent superintendents have allowed me the privilege of climbing up to the torch periodically to help my full-time replacement with maintenance. Even as a volunteer, my love for Lady Liberty—and for all the freedom, justice and hope that she stands for—has continued. I cannot thank God enough for answering my prayer as a visitor to the statue in 1968 and for allowing me the privilege of serving Lady Liberty as the "Keeper of the Flame" for so many years.

THIS BOOK WAS MADE POSSIBLE BY THE COLLABORATIVE EFFORTS OF THE FOLLOWING PARTNERS:

The National Park Service preserves unimpaired the natural and cultural resources and values of the National Park System for the enjoyment, education, and inspiration of this and future generations. The National Park Service cooperates with partners to extend the benefits of natural and cultural resource preservation and outdoor recreation throughout the United States.

www.nps.gov

Eastern National—a not-for-profit partner of the National Park Service for over 60 years—provides quality products and services to visitors of America's national parks and other public trusts. Headquartered outside of Philadelphia, PA, the organization has donated over $89 million to the National Park Service to support interpretive and educational programs. Eastern National operates museum shops in parks throughout the United States, helping visitors better understand the parks and their resources. Each year, Eastern National donates its profits to the National Park Service to support park programs. Your purchases in park visitor centers support park education programs! Shop online at www.eParks.com

www.easternnational.org

Employees & Alumni Association
of the National Park Service

The heart of the National Park Service is its employees; the dedicated, 20,000-plus strong workforce that maintains, interprets, protects and manages our national parks. The Employees & Alumni Association of the National Park Service (E&AA) is a membership organization dedicated to promoting the values and ideals of the National Park Service. The E&AA membership is a diverse group of current employees, alumni, volunteers and other interested partners who see the National Park Service, and its family, as important parts of their lives. E&AA members are dedicated to the mission and work of the National Park Service.

www.eandaa.org

As Ford Motor Company celebrates its long-time partnership with the National Park Foundation and the National Park Service, we remain committed to founder Henry Ford's dream to provide every American with the means to enjoy "...happy hours spent in God's great open spaces". Today, as a Proud Partner of America's National Parks, Ford continues to believe in supporting and protecting these special places that all Americans can share, experience, learn from and enjoy.

www.ford.com

American Park Network publishes the world's largest outdoor guides, read by over 20 million national park enthusiasts each year. Its mission to support national parks and public lands has been a driving force for more than two decades. The publication of *Oh, Ranger!* is just one example of the meaningful results that can be achieved through creative public/ private partnerships. This book would not have been possible without the collaborative efforts of all the partners listed here. Hopefully this project will serve as inspiration for new partnerships that will help preserve our natural and cultural resources, unimpaired for the enjoyment of future generations.

www.americanparknetwork.com